Early American History

A LITERATURE APPROACH FOR 7TH-9TH GRADE

Early American History, A Literature Approach for 7th - 9th Grade
by Rebecca Manor © 2021
All rights reserved.
Published by Beautiful Feet Books
ISBN 978-1893103931
Layout and Design by Ryan Maloney

Table of Contents

How to Use This Guide

Welcome to the fascinating world of American history. Covering over a thousand years, this study encompasses Native cultures, the Age of Discovery, colonial settlements, revolution, slavery, the Trail of Tears, and much more. It may seem daunting to cover all this history in a year, but this guide is your tool, designed to educate and delight your student.

Grade Level and Overview: This is a one-year study appropriate for 7th through 9th grade, inspired by the Charlotte Mason method of education: reading, reasoning, relating, and recording. The heart of this study is the great literature selections. Exploring the world through story is often one of the most cherished experiences shared by homeschooling families. The development of critical reasoning and research skills begins to be very important at this age. Students are at a developmental stage that allows them to see events from more than one perspective. Cultivating this skill encourages deeper thinking, empathy, and curiosity.

Content: Livy, the ancient Roman historian, said:

> *"What makes the study of history so valuable, is the fact that you can behold, displayed as on a monument, every kind of conduct. Thence you may select for yourself and your country, that which you may imitate, thence note what is shameful in the undertaking, and shameful in the result, which you may avoid."*

As Livy notes so well, there are triumphal and disappointing events in history. While this study covers hard topics, it does so with age-appropriate detail, recognizing that as students mature there will be ample opportunity for expanding their knowledge. This gives you, the teacher, the option to choose when that time comes. Topics like slavery and the mistreatment of Native Peoples are covered both for historical accuracy and to help cultivate compassion and empathy. The resources in Rabbit Trails offer curated selections to expand on these topics. When the readings include especially detailed depictions of violence or offensive terms, those have been noted in the lessons.

Many assignments include research on a variety of perspectives and viewpoints. This may expose students to new ideas that they will need to grapple with in order to reach their own conclusions. Encourage your student to discuss their findings and how their perspectives are being shaped. Push them to seek out reputable sources as they research and to resist easy explanations.

Historical perceptions of unknown or unfamiliar cultures and people change over time as knowledge and respect overcome ignorance and prejudice. This process repeats itself throughout history and is preserved in historical documents and texts. Rewriting and erasing this evidence to suit modern taste does not provide the opportunities for correction and instruction we believe are such a valuable aspect of learning history. Recognizing human brokenness and seeing the failings of the past is part of the reason we study history, and we see the hard parts of it as inescapable and valuable in the lessons they teach. As you read through the literature included in this study, you will encounter a few instances where these historical attitudes and descriptions will be offensive. We have provided discussion questions to help you navigate these topics as well as content warnings on specific lessons.

Pace: This study contains 82 lessons; if you are planning on the standard 180-day school year, complete two lessons each week. If you are teaching younger students or using it across a range of ages, work at your own pace. There is no pre-set schedule. When life gets busy or the holidays are approaching, slow down. If your students are intrigued by a certain subject, follow those rabbit trails. Our guides are designed to support your teaching style, not dictate it. One of the greatest gifts of homeschooling is the flexibility and freedom that is built into setting your own schedule. This teacher guide is designed to be a tool, not a taskmaster.

Activities: This guide includes some recommended hands-on activities. We also link to websites that have further activities. None of these are required. Do what adds enjoyment to your study.

Student Portfolio: Each student should have a notebook or portfolio that they are comfortable working with. This may be a simple notebook. It could also be a blog or an art folder. All written work, drawings, reports, and mapping activities are to be added to this portfolio.

Narration and Discussion Prompts: As you read through the literature with your students, use the questions to help spur conversation and verbal processing unless you are following a strict Charlotte Mason narration model. The discussion questions are designed for conversation and to encourage critical thinking and reasoning skills. These are not comprehension questions, and therefore answer keys are not provided. If you are unable to read along with your student, these questions will allow you to discuss the topics and ideas your student encounters in the reading. Feel free to ask clarifying questions of your student. The included questions are simply a starting point. Let conversation and processing proceed naturally and encourage it by asking your own questions.

Websites: Throughout the study, you will find a curated selection of websites. These specific website pages have all been viewed and deemed appropriate and accurate at the time of printing. Potentially objectionable material has been noted. The recommendation of one page on a website is not an endorsement of the entire contents of that website. Students should always use the internet with care and under adult supervision. Type in the address as it appears to find the correct information. If a web link is no longer working, don't give up. Simply use the words in the web address to guide your search. You may also check for updated links for this guide here: www.bfbooks.com/Teacher-Guide-Website-Links

Rabbit Trails: At the beginning of each section, you will find a list of additional recommended books to check out from your local library. None of these titles are required. We provide these lists in order to help you sift through the hundreds of books available on the many topics covered in this study. However, if you have a voracious reader or if a certain topic proves especially interesting, these curated selections will give your student the opportunity to choose titles for themselves. This empowers them to develop agency in their own education.

Creative Writing Prompt: Each section includes a creative writing prompt inspired by one of the literature selections. Use these for students who want to develop their storytelling or creative writing skills. These are not required and are simply provided for fun.

Research Topics: There are research topics in each section. Students should choose one in each section and write a research paper. You may download a free grading rubric from www.bfbooks.com/Info-FAQ/Free-Downloads. These topics can also be used for discussions, presentations, debates, etc.

World History: The emphasis of this study is on North American history, concentrating on the United States. If you would like to add a world history overview, we have included tables at the back of this manual to facilitate using Genevieve Foster's "World" titles to do so.

Map: A large, durable, outline map of North America is required for this course. Your student may draw his or her own map on heavy-weight cardstock, download a template online, or purchase the map available here: www.bfbooks.com/USA-Colonies-Map

Do I Have to Do Everything in Every Lesson? No! Again, this is a tool, not a taskmaster. Everything in this guide is provided to make your job easier and save you time. Every lesson, assignment, and activity is here to help you expand the literature, pull out historical content, and provide structure and guidance, but feel free to skip steps when it suits your family.

Lastly, share your work on social media and tag us at **#beautifulfeetbooks**. We love seeing your creativity.

Literature Used in This Study

Indigenous Peoples of North America & First Encounters

The World Made New
by Marc Aronson and John W. Glenn

Peacemaker
by Joseph Bruchac

The Early Colonial Period: 1607–1706

The World of Capt. John Smith
written and illustrated by Genevieve Foster

Pocahontas
by Joseph Bruchac

Almost Home
by Wendy Lawton

The Later Colonial Period: 1706–1776

The Kidnapped Prince: The Life of Olaudah Equiano
by Olaudah Equiano, adapted by Ann Cameron

Poor Richard
by James Daugherty

George Washington's World
written and illustrated by Genevieve Foster

The Revolutionary War: 1776–1783

Sophia's War
by Avi

Black Heroes of the American Revolution
By Burke Davis

The Young United States: 1783–1864

Fever 1793
by Laurie Halse Anderson

Carry On, Mr. Bowditch
by Jean Lee Latham

Of Courage Undaunted, Across the Continent with Lewis & Clark
by James Daugherty

Abraham Lincoln's World
written and illustrated by Genevieve Foster

Mary and the Trail of Tears, A Cherokee Removal Survival Story
by Andrea L. Rogers

Sojourner Truth, Ain't I a Woman?
by Patricia C. McKissack and Fredrick McKissack

PART I

The Indigenous Peoples of North America and First Encounters

Sinagua dwelling at Montezuma Castle National Monument, Camp Verde, Arizona

As we embark on this course, we will begin with the first people groups in North America. For a long time, we did not know a lot about these nations because much of the archaeological evidence had been eroded, lost, or destroyed. Thankfully, scholars, archaeologists, and Native storytellers have been working tirelessly to restore the record. Stories passed down through oral traditions are being recorded and published, filling in details we cannot obtain strictly through excavations. In addition, important sites are now protected and studied using archaeological methods, giving us a picture of how people lived, what they ate, and how they worshipped and governed.

People groups settled throughout North America, and when Columbus first landed, some scholars make the case that up to 100 million people lived in the Americas. These nations and tribes established villages, cities, governments, religious practices, agricultural systems, and civilizations. Nations went to war, empires rose and fell, people groups flourished, and some disappeared. Just as countries grew and faltered in ancient and medieval Europe, Asia, and Africa, the same pattern of history was working itself out in North and South America.

The Native Peoples of North America were responsible for remarkable achievements in architecture, transportation, medicine, agriculture, and government. For example, Cahokia, a mound city built on the banks of the Mississippi, was larger than London in 1250 AD. The Mississippians were accomplished builders and created public works and mound structures that rivaled the great pyramids of ancient Egypt.

In California, the Ohlone developed a system of controlled burns that yielded agricultural advances while reducing the risk of wildfires. On the East Coast, Wampanoag and Iroquois created food forests through intercropping. Many people groups relied on the Three Sisters—corn, beans, and squash—as their staple crops. The beans and squash were planted amid the corn, growing up the stalks and providing ground cover to limit weed growth. The Powhatan, or Algonquin-speaking people, cultivated tobacco nearly 1500 years ago. Ice-fishing and maple syrup are both Native inventions.

The Native Peoples' respect for their environments led to the development of a broad knowledge of the medicinal properties of plants and roots, allowing them to treat many common illnesses effectively. The lack of domesticated animals also limited their exposure to animal-borne illnesses, protecting them from these diseases until the Europeans and their farm animals arrived. At that point, diseases like smallpox ran rampant through many Native tribes who had not developed natural immunities, resulting in the deaths of millions of people.

Excavated artifacts from distances as far away as 1000 miles show extensive trade networks between nations and tribes. These trade routes depended on various styles of canoes fashioned from local trees such as birch, redwood, and more. Canoes ranged from agile single-person vessels to large pitched boats that could carry up to 20 men.

Governmental systems were often egalitarian and centered on each tribal member being given a voice. Listening to others was highly valued. Most tribes governed with an eye toward the future, some even looking seven generations into the future to ensure that any action they took would be beneficial for their great-great-great-grandchildren. This forward-thinking approach resulted in the Iroquois Confederacy, a league of Native nations and tribes that still exists today! It even inspired the Articles of Confederation and the U.S. Constitution. Benjamin Franklin's admonition that the 13 colonies form a "voluntary union" was inspired by his knowledge of this confederacy. We will learn more about this in the book *Peacemaker* by Joseph Bruchac.

As we read through this section, seek out local resources to learn about the tribes that lived in your area. There are probably local museums dedicated to preserving the cultures and traditions they have passed down to their descendants. See if you can learn more about your local tribes at powwows.com. We also encourage you to use the Rabbit Trails and resources listed in this section to explore further.

In this section, we will be learning about several Native nations, the Iroquois Confederacy, and the first European explorers of the Americas.

Rabbit Trails //

Before Columbus: The Americas of 1491 by Charles C. Mann
Building from archeological artifacts and DNA evidence, the story of Indigenous Peoples in the Americas becomes ever more complex and fascinating. From genetic engineering of maize to remarkable structures like the Cahokia Mounds, America's first inhabitants' stories make up a valuable part of our American heritage.

Beyond the Sea of Ice: The Voyages of Henry Hudson
by Joan Elizabeth Goodman
Henry Hudson's stubborn desire to find a northern passage to Asia resulted in four harrowing voyages that tested him and his men beyond all reason.

Despite All Obstacles: La Salle and the Conquest of the Mississippi
by Joan Elizabeth Goodman
"In Adversity he was never cast down and always hoped with the help of heaven to succeed in his enterprises despite all the obstacles that rose against it." This quote from the *Chronicle of La Salle's Last Expedition* demonstrates the obstinate, visionary, and bullheaded persistence of the French explorer.

The Earth Under Sky Bear's Feet:
Native American Poems of the Land
by Joseph Bruchac and Thomas Locker
Beautiful illustrations accompany poems retelling traditional Native myths and stories from a variety of tribes and nations.

Gift Horse: A Lakota Story by S. D. Nelson
As a Standing Rock Sioux tribe member, Nelson drew inspiration for this story from his great-great-grandfather. Young Flying Cloud and his horse Storm go through tests of stamina, courage, and faithfulness.

The Girl Who Helped Thunder:
And Other Native American Folktales by Joseph Bruchac
Turtle Island: The Story of North America's First People
by Eldon Yellowhorn and Kathy Lowinger
Both anthologies present traditional folktales and myths of America's Indigenous people, teaching humility and gratitude.

The Golden Flower: A Taino Myth from Puerto Rico
by Nina Jaffe, illustrated by Enrique Sanches
This lovely picture book relates the Taino creation myth and shows the importance of the pumpkin to Caribbean cultures.

Character Connection //

HOSPITALITY: Have your student define hospitality using the dictionary. Discuss the meaning of hospitality as it pertains to these verses. Does Biblical hospitality differ from the dictionary's definition of hospitality? If so, in what ways?

Hebrews 13:1-2
Hebrews 13:16
1 Peter 4:8-9
Romans 12:12-18
Leviticus 19:33-34
Galatians 5:13
Matthew 25:40
Proverbs 31:20
John 13:3-16

As you read through the literature in this section, take note of events that demonstrate hospitality. Consider what provoked hospitable behavior. Was it to treat others with dignity and love or out of a desire to gain something?

Write about a time when someone showed radical hospitality to you and your family. List some ways that you can practice hospitality. Choose one from your list and implement it. Often it is as simple as smiling at someone, opening a door, or saying good morning.

APPLICATION:

- Take a prayer walk around your neighborhood.
- Bake a sweet treat and deliver it to a neighbor.
- Prepare dinner for a family that is going through a hard time.

Indians written and illustrated by Edwin Tunis
Mr. Tunis has re-created here, in spectacular detail, every meaningful aspect of a past way of life. The author's devotion to honoring and recording the customs, arts, and traditions in 245 accurate drawings is a treasure store that continues to speak over 60 years after its original publication.

The Sea-Ringed World: Sacred Stories of the Americas
by María García Esperón, illustrated by Amanda Mijangos, translated by David Bowles
This beautifully illustrated compilation of creation myths, legends, fables, and stories from many American Native traditions is a must-have for anyone who finds ancient mythologies fascinating.

Trickster: Native American Tales, A Graphic Collection
This collection of stories from Native writers and illustrators is a good resource for those looking to explore ancestral myths and beliefs.

We Asked for Nothing: The Remarkable Journey of Cabeza de Vaca by Stuart Waldman
In 1528 the conquistador Alvar Núñez Cabeza de Vaca was shipwrecked on Texas's coast and rescued by Karankawa Indians. For eight years, he shared life with various Southwestern tribes and survived because of them. Returning to Spain, De Vaca became an advocate for the New World's Indigenous people. Highly recommended.

Where the Buffaloes Begin by Olaf Baker and illustrated by Stephen Gammell
Olaf Baker's first-person account of life among the Blackfoot captures the strength, resilience, and independence of this Indigenous tribe.

The World of Columbus and Sons by Genevieve Foster
The age of discovery changed the world, and this book shows how. Covering events around the world during the lifetime of Christopher Columbus, this book lets readers travel from Europe to Asia and North and South America and Africa to meet the people who shaped the world during this pivotal time.

Online Resources //

Explore native plants and how Indigenous peoples used them. The following resource provides a wealth of information and is worth printing out. Visit www.tomaquagmuseum.org/resources and scroll down and click on "Indigenous Garden at KettlePond Visitor's Center Curriculum" to access the PDF.

Celebrate Native Culture today: Watch "6 Stories Celebrating Native American History and Culture" on the Great Big Story YouTube channel.

PBS offers a wealth of information on Native American history and culture. Check it out here:
www.pbs.org/show/native-america/

What was it like to be a sailor in the 15th century? Find out here:
www.rmg.co.uk/stories/topics/life-sea-age-sail

Research Topics //

INTERNATIONAL ALLIANCES Compare the founding and purposes of the Iroquois League of Peace with another voluntary international alliance like the United Nations, NATO, the League of Nations, or the G8. Why did the nations and leaders seek unification, and what was accomplished by forming a united governing body? Compare the benefits and drawbacks.

LEGACY Write a paper tracing the history of the Iroquois League of Peace from its founding to now. How has this alliance helped preserve these nations when so many others were extinguished through conquest, disease, and warfare? What is the role of the League today?

Activities & Handicraft //

MAPPING: Mapping and navigation were essential skills for the explorers who ventured across unknown seas to uncharted lands. Hone your mapping and geolocation skills with the following activities:

> http://naturemappingfoundation.org/natmap/education/protocols/6_mapping_part1.html
> http://naturemappingfoundation.org/natmap/education/protocols/6_mapping_part2.html
>
> www.edutopia.org/naturemapping-lesson-maps-directions-coordinates

Every European explorer relied on his compass. Make your own using the instructions below:

> www.nps.gov/articles/compass.htm

LONGHOUSES: Use the instructions found on the following website to build your own longhouse, either life-sized or a model.

> www.nysm.nysed.gov/exhibitions/ongoing/native-peoples-new-york/mohawk-longhouse.

BASKET WEAVING: Native artisans passed down the art of basket weaving for hundreds of years. Learn more about traditional Haudenosaunee designs here:

> www.snpolytechnic.com/sites/default/files/docs/resource/13_basket_making_lesson.pdf

Explore basket designs from all over North America:
> www.native-languages.org/baskets.htm
> www.nativetech.org/basketry/index.html

Try your hand at weaving a basket via the following links.

Traditional Native American basket

> Make a pine needle basket:
> "Making a Basket from PINE NEEDLES |
> Start to Finish Project" on the Wild She Goes
> YouTube channel
>
> Woven basket project, with a printable template:
> www.craftpassion.com/easy-basket-weaving/

"Quick and Easy Blackberry Bramble Basket" on the PacoWarabi YouTube channel.

POTTERY: Nearly every culture has had some form of pottery, and examples exist throughout the ancient civilizations of North America. Make your own using the instructions at the following sites:
> www.education.com/activity/article/easy-clay-pinch-pots
> www.teachersfirst.com/lessons/nativecrafts/pinchpot.cfm

Creative Writing Prompt //

Storytelling has been central to the human experience for all of history. The story of the Iroquois League of Peace is part of an ongoing and robust storytelling tradition among the Haudenosaunee people. Stories tell us where we come from, what we believe, and what we hold dear. They also tell us about other people, who they are, and what they believe. Over the next two weeks, write a story that communicates some aspect of who you are. This can be an account of an important event in your life or a story you make up. Partner with a friend or classmate to share your stories. What do the stories tell you about your partner? Do they help you understand him or her better?

LESSON 1

If you have not already done so, please read How to Use This Guide, on page 2, before embarking on this journey of historical discovery.

1. 1492 stands out as a year in which two worlds met for the first time, setting a torrent of change into motion. To understand how world-changing that year was, we need to look back further to the people who already lived in what would become known as the Americas. We will also read about some ideas and movements that led to Columbus setting out on that historic voyage. Introduce The World Made New by Marc Aronson and John W. Glenn. Read the Introduction and pages 6-19. Discussion prompt:

> The causes behind the Age of Exploration included religious zeal and a desire for new converts, competition between rival European kingdoms, the search for wealth, the desire for glory, and increased knowledge of the physical world. Choose one cause to explore and trace how it led to world-changing consequences. Keep in mind that many of these ideas connect. For example, Columbus desired fame, wealth, and converts to Christianity. He was shaped by the passionate religious fervor behind the Crusades and the expulsion of the Moors from Spain, his humble background, and his great ambition. These were motivating factors (or causes) behind his desire to sail west to reach the East. Discuss the connection between ideas and action.

2. To learn more about the two worlds that met in 1492, watch "America Before Columbus," a documentary produced by National Geographic and available on various sites, including Vimeo, YouTube, or on DVD from many local libraries.

3. Draw or purchase a large outline map of North America. Beautiful Feet offers one here:
www.bfbooks.com/USA-Colonies-Map
Or draw your own using heavy-weight cardstock to ensure the map lasts the whole school year. On the map of North America, mark the following landmarks, referring to an atlas if necessary:

Atlantic Ocean	Caribbean Sea	Gulf of Mexico
Mississippi River	Illinois River	Missouri River
Lake Michigan	Lake Huron	Lake Erie
Lake Superior	Lake Ontario	Cahokia
St. Louis, Missouri		

4. To learn more about American cultures before Columbus, visit the following website, viewing a section or two each day throughout this section of our study:

www.khanacademy.org/humanities/us-history/precontact-and-early-colonial-era/before-contact/v/native-american-societies-before-contact

5. Begin a new section in your portfolio titled: Indigenous Peoples of North America. Record any facts and findings you deem significant as you progress through this section's readings and assignments.

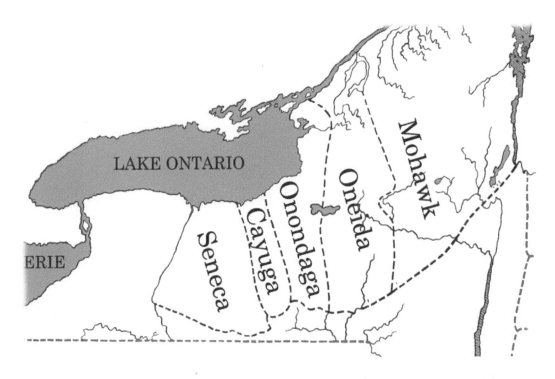

1. Iroquois Nations, c. 1142
2. Leaders from five Iroquois nations assembled around Dekanawidah c. 1570, French engraving, early 18th century.

LESSON 2

1. We will now read about one of the nations that have long existed in North America, the Iroquois, or Haudenosaunee. Introduce *Peacemaker* by Joseph Bruchac. This story is set in the 14th century, southeast of Lake Ontario. It records the founding of the oldest living (or ongoing) participatory democracy in the world, a story that has been passed down through generation after generation of Iroquois storytellers. Read Chapters 1-4. Discussion prompts:

> Describe the relationships between the tribes and nations surrounding Kanata.

> Describe the scene where Tawis and Okwaho are attacked. How do you think you would have reacted if you were in their place?

> Describe Okwaho and Tawis's attitudes toward Clouds Forming's challenges. How can this mindset reframe obstacles or hardship?

2. Using the map at the beginning of *Peacemaker* as your guide, mark the territories and lands of the five tribes that make up the Iroquois Nation near Lake Ontario on your map of North America. See left for reference.

3. Within the Indigenous Peoples section of your portfolio, create a section titled "The Iroquois Confederacy." Place all assignments related to the Iroquois and your readings in *Peacemaker* here.

4. The Iroquois game tewaraathon (mentioned on page 29 of *Peacemaker*) was played by many Native nations. Research the history of this game, and record your findings in your portfolio. What did tewaraathon eventually become? *Lacrosse.*

5. Begin working on a project from the Handicraft section.

LESSON 3

1. Read Chapters 5-8 of *Peacemaker*. Discussion prompts:

> Narrate the story "The Twins" as told by Okwaho's mother, Wolf Woman.

> Long before the phrase "listen to understand" was coined, the Onondaga people practiced this art. Discuss the importance of listening for understanding and how it differs from listening for the purpose of debate. How did the Onondaga structure their culture to encourage listening? How had Atatarho strayed from this central practice?

> Describe how anger grows inside Okwaho and changes the way he views everything around him.

2. Record your narration of "The Twins" in your notebook, along with a reflection on what this story tells us about the values and beliefs of the Onondaga people.

3. Learn more about how the longhouse was central to Iroquois life by watching "The People of the Longhouse" on the Nicholas Varga YouTube channel. Also, visit:
> www.nysm.nysed.gov/exhibitions/ongoing/native-peoples-new-york/mohawk-longhouse.

4. Continue working on your handicraft project.

LESSON 4

1. Read Chapters 9-12 of *Peacemaker*. **Parental Warning:** Chapter 10 tells the story of a grandmother repeatedly trying to kill her infant grandson through exposure because she believes he is evil. Sensitive students may find this disturbing. Discussing the following topics before this chapter is read may be helpful: the idea of unwanted children, the historical practice of exposing infants, and spiritual beliefs that include possession by evil spirits. Christianity was the first world religion to view children as inherently valuable and worthy of respect and care. Jesus' acceptance of children was revolutionary and countercultural to the ancient world's low view of the young. Discussion prompts:

> The Peacemaker's birth contains several elements similar to those of the Biblical account of Jesus' birth: virgin birth, resurrection, child born as a gift from the Creator to bring peace to earth. These similarities are an example of "common grace," or the idea that God provides truth to all people in all cultures. Discuss these similarities in light of the view that all truth is God's truth. What are some key differences between the stories?

> These chapters include stories that have been told for nearly a thousand years of Iroquois history. Choose one to narrate, and record it in your portfolio. Discuss why your choice stood out to you and what it tells us about the Iroquois people.

> Discuss how hope calmed Okwaho's anger.

2. Continue working your way through the articles on Native American cultures from Khan Academy: www.khanacademy.org/humanities/us-history/precontact-and-early-colonial-era/before-contact/v/native-american-societies-before-contact

3. Continue working on your handicraft project, or if you have finished, choose a new one.

LESSON 5

1. Finish reading *Peacemaker*. Discussion prompt:

> Embracing peace came at a significant cost to Hiawatha. Discuss how giving up his right to avenge his daughters' death and forgiving Atatarho was a sacrifice for a greater good.

2. Read more about the Iroquois League of Peace and how it helped shape the United States Constitution. www.history.com/news/iroquois-confederacy-influence-us-constitution

3. Draw or paint a scene from a favorite story or event in *Peacemaker*. Add to the portfolio.

Early Localization of Native Americans

1. Battle between Iroquois and Algonquin tribes near Lake Champlain as drawn by Samuel de Champlain, 1613
2. Iroquois with western goods pictured in *Histoire de l'Amérique septentrionale: divisée en quatre tomes* by Bacqueville de la Potherie recounting his travels in the Great Lakes and Mississippi regions at the end of the 17th century.

LESSON 6

1. Conclude your study of the Iroquois, or the Haudenosaunee people, with a written reflection on the history of the League of Peace. Consider its importance in world history, what ideas led to it, and how those ideas went on to influence world history.

2. Oral tradition and art, specifically wampum, carried the Iroquois League of Peace story through history across geography and cultures. Learn more via the following links:

    www.onondaganation.org/culture/wampum/
    www.pbs.org/video/traditional-wampum-belts-gy05in/

3. Over the next few days, explore other Native cultures. Check out local Native and historical organizations and museums, as they will have the best information on historical and current tribes in your area. Below you will find resources and documentaries. These sites, along with the Rabbit Trails recommendations, will be helpful. Keep in mind that there are many more resources available at libraries and online. Searching for those will help hone your research skills.

    General Information
        "Pre Columbian Americas | World History | Khan Academy" on the Khan Academy YouTube channel

    Mound Builders
        www.nps.gov/nr/travel/mounds/builders.htm

        "Inside the Secret Mounds of Pre-Historic America | Ancient Mysteries (S3) | Full Episode | History" on the History YouTube channel

    Native Tribes of the Southwest
        "Native Peoples of the Southwest - Exploring Our Past on the Learning Videos Channel" on the Harmony Square YouTube channel

        www.nps.gov/meve/learn/historyculture/cliff_dwellings_home.htm

        www.legendsofamerica.com/na-puebloindians/

4. Finish working on your handicraft project.

LESSON 7

1. Read pages 20-35 of *The World Made New*. Choose one explorer featured on these pages to research further over the next two days and record your findings in the portfolio.

2. Voices of the Past on YouTube has produced videos narrating primary sources from Natives and European explorers during the Age of Discovery. Each video contains an advertisement for the producer's subscription service at some point in the narration. Just continue watching until the narration continues. **Parental Warning:** These primary documents have accounts of violence, drunkenness, torture, and other historical realities. Check out the following videos, all found on the Voices of the Past YouTube channel:

    "Leif Erikson discovers America // 999 AD // The Saga of Erik the Red"
    "Inca Perspective on FIRST CONTACT with Europeans // Account of Titu Cusi (1570) // Primary Source"
    "Aztec Perspective on First Contact with Europeans // 16th cent. Florentine Codex // Primary Source"
    "Cortés Meets Montezuma // Cortés' letters // 8th November 1519"

1. Traditional Native American food 2. The Three Sisters: squash, corn, and beans

LESSON 8

1. Read pages 36-53 of *The World Made New*. Discussion prompt:

> What do you think about drawing parallels between Columbus's voyage and the idea that it was equivalent to discovering life on another planet? The five centuries that separate us from 1492 have both clouded the sharpness of this change and increased our understanding of this historical moment's magnitude. We know that Columbus never truly understood the world he had come to, only thinking of it as a barrier to his dream of reaching Asia. Only the passage of decades and centuries would accurately reveal the epic proportions of this global collision.

2. Finish research on your chosen explorer and record the report in the portfolio.

3. To conclude this section, host a feast featuring Native recipes. During the event, you could relate a favorite Iroquois story from *Peacemaker* and present what you have learned about the Native Peoples of North America. Research recipes from local tribes or use the following links:

> Iroquois white corn recipes:
> https://ganondagan.org/whitecorn/recipes
>
> Sioux chef uses indigenous ingredients to create beautiful recipes:
> www.cowboysindians.com/2017/10/the-sioux-chefs-indigenous-kitchen/
>
> Make poyha, a traditional cornmeal meatloaf:
> www.food.com/recipe/poyha-old-native-american-recipe-meat-cormeal-174079
>
> Scrumptious salad made of the Three Sisters:
> https://festival.si.edu/blog/native-recipe-three-sisters-salad
>
> Ohlone salad using native plants and other ingredients:
> www.pbs.org/food/native-america/make-ohlone-salad/
>
> Cherokee bean bread:
> www.pbs.org/food/native-america/discover-traditional-cherokee-bean-bread/

4. The following video provides a detailed but helpful summary of what we have just studied: "The Age of Exploration: Crash Course European History #4" on the CrashCourse YouTube channel.

PART II

The
Early Colonial Period
1607–1706

*E*uropean exploration of North America instigated a flurry of activity across the Atlantic. The endless bounds of the sea were conquered, and now the horizon was a beacon of limitless possibility instead of unknown terror. As reports trickled back to Europe, often replete with exaggeration and legend, they found an eager audience.

Listless or bored aristocrats signed on to expeditions expecting to find treasure, fame, and adventure. Tenant farmers saw an opportunity to lay claim to land of their own. Artisans and merchants recognized emerging markets for their goods and services. Refugees from the endless conflicts that plagued Europe sought peace. Victims of religious oppression desired to worship in freedom or establish theocracies where their rights were protected.

The reasons for embarking on a risky journey to the "new world" were varied, but nearly all the settlers faced extreme hardship during the voyage and when they landed. Despite this reality, the colonization efforts of Spain, France, England, the Dutch Republic, and other European nations grew throughout the late 16th and 17th centuries. As we saw earlier in this study, what many Europeans saw as a vast "virgin" territory was already settled by Native tribes and nations. This did not hinder those who sought to claim land for themselves.

England concentrated its energies on the northeastern seaboard, and the Spanish raised their flag in Florida and along the Gulf of Mexico. France explored the vast Louisiana Territory, and the Dutch established New Amsterdam in what would eventually become New York.

As more permanent colonies took hold, the Native populations were pushed further west, and tensions grew, often overflowing into violent massacres on both sides. Some colonists genuinely sought to build positive relationships with the tribes they lived near. William Penn, the Pilgrims, and James Oglethorpe in Georgia all maintained mutually beneficial relationships with local tribes for years. Sadly, these periods of peace gave way to aggressive land grabs fueled by increased settlement. Native tribes were displaced, and their lands were stolen over decades and centuries.

We will learn about the high points and the low points of this period, which saw rapid growth in the colonies, the establishment of a fiercely independent middle class, and an expanding appreciation for freedom that would have world-changing consequences. Let's begin in Jamestown, established as an English colony on May 4, 1607.

Rabbit Trails //

Blood on the River: James Town 1607 by Elsa Carbone

Samuel Collier, a London street urchin arrested for stealing something that rightfully belongs to him, finds a second chance as Captain John Smith's page boy. Samuel's perspective provides context to the class tensions between the settlers, hostilities between the English and the Powhatan, and Captain John Smith's leadership.

Blue Birds by Caroline Starr Rose

Alis, an English lass settling in the colony of Roanoke, has little in common with Kimi, a Roanoke girl, but the two strike up an unlikely friendship. Alternating poems from each girl communicate their growing attachment amid increased suspicion between the settlers and the Natives. Questions of authority and obedience are explored within the context of a friendship that defies all warnings and admonitions against it.

Mourt's Relation: A Journal of the Pilgrims at Plymouth
Of Plymouth Plantation by William Bradford

These primary sources provide most of the information we have on the Pilgrims' journey and first years in Plymouth.

Witches! The Absolutely True Tale of Disaster in Salem written and illustrated by Rosalyn Schanzer

If you've ever wondered what happened during the Salem Witch Trials, this book traces the story from a minister's young daughters to the tragic hanging of over 20 people in early colonial Massachusetts. *Parental Warning*: Preview content for sensitive readers.

The Witch of Blackbird Pond by Elizabeth George Speare

This Newbery Medal winner has long been a favorite book for exploring the religious complexities and tensions that existed in the early colonial days. Kit Tyler has only known the warmth of her Caribbean home and now must face the literal and cultural cold of her relatives' Puritan community. Delving beyond surface appearances, Speare examines suspicion, ignorance, and prejudice in this engaging novel.

The World of William Penn by Genevieve Foster, edited by Rea Berg

Genevieve Foster explores the wide world of William Penn, a world reaching across the courtyards of the Sun King to the Great Wall of China. Penn's contemporaries included such colorful figures as Louis XIV, Peter the Great, Edmund Halley, Sir Isaac Newton, Shah Jahan (who built the Taj Mahal), and the great explorers Marquette, Jolliet, and La Salle. Penn's life spans a fascinating age of exploration and discovery.

Character Connection //

WISDOM: Discuss wisdom and your understanding of this virtue. Describe its characteristics and its benefits. Compare the definition you formed through discussion to a dictionary definition. What are some synonyms and antonyms of wisdom? Write the definition of wisdom in your portfolio.

Read James 1:5 and James 3:17.

As you read through the literature in this section, record quotes that express wisdom in your portfolio. Discuss them in light of the Bible verses above.

Online Resources //

The Historic Jamestowne website provides a wealth of information on the English settlement and Powhatan culture.

https://historicjamestowne.org/

Khan Academy has an excellent unit on colonial America with informative video lectures, articles, and more. Use these to add context and background information to our literary selections.

www.khanacademy.org/humanities/us-history/colonial-america

Activities & Handicraft //

BUILD JAMESTOWN: Build a model of the Jamestown settlement. There are several options linked below:

> Printable model for purchase:
> https://store.homeschoolinthewoods.com/products/the-jamestown-replica-3d-project

> Lego Jamestown inspiration: https://inpursuitofwildthings.blog/2013/09/20/pocahontas-and-jamestown-with-beautiful-feet-books-and-lego-jamestown/

> Build Jamestown in Minecraft: https://education.minecraft.net/content/minecraft-edu/language-masters/en-us/lessons.html/jamestown-settlement

ARCHERY: Learn about Powhatan bows and arrows:

> "Primed and Loaded | Introduction to the Powhatan Bow" on JYF Museums YouTube channel

> Build a bow! There are a variety of instructional videos at all skill levels available on YouTube

GROW TULIPS: In honor of the Pilgrims' time in Holland, sprout tulips in a jar! Bulbs can be purchased year-round at garden shops or online. Follow the instruction at the following links:

> www.gardeningknowhow.com/ornamental/bulbs/tulips/growing-tulips-in-water.htm

> https://tulipsinholland.com/2014/12/grow-tulips-in-glass-jars/

COOK WAMPANOAG FOOD: The following website contains a wealth of Wampanoag recipes:
www.manyhoops.com/wampanoag-food-and-recipes_1.html

Creative Writing Prompt //

Create a newspaper for the Jamestown settlement. Include stories and interviews that capture life in the colony, the conflicts and challenges. Letters to the editor are a clever way to include multiple perspectives. And, of course, comics are a fun element.

Research Topics //

HISTORICAL RECORD-KEEPING: Captain John Smith recorded and published *The Generall Historie of Virginia, New-England, and the Summer Isles*, and this work set the tone for how Jamestown was remembered. The Powhatan passed their histories of this time period down through generations of storytellers. Compare and contrast these two methods of recording history.

FAITH AND POLITICS: Write a paper about how the Christian faith of the Jamestown settlers' guided, or failed to guide, their interactions with the Powhatan. Read Acts 17:16-33. How did Paul model observing and engaging in culture? How could the settlers have behaved differently if they had allowed Paul's example to guide their actions? When did they act in a way that expressed Christian love for their neighbors?

CHANGING HISTORY: For centuries, Smith's account of Pocahontas saving his life guided historians' understanding of this pivotal event. We now know that the Powhatans' account is very different. Research and compare both versions. What assumptions and misunderstandings are corrected when you consider both perspectives?

Incolarum Virginiae piscandi ratio (*The Method of Fishing of the Inhabitants of Virginia*)
by Theodor de Bry after John White, c. 1590.

LESSON 9

1. Mark the following on the map of North America:

    Jamestown, Virginia   Roanoke Colony   Chesapeake Bay
    Potomac River

2. As we learned in *The World Made New*, many European powers were nearly frantic to stake a claim in the Americas. We've had an overview of the leading explorers and will now focus on English efforts in North America, as these settlements became the colonies that eventually became the founding states. First, we must cross the Atlantic and familiarize ourselves with what was going on in England at the time. Introduce *The World of Capt. John Smith* by Genevieve Foster. Read pages viii-11, 21-22, and 32-38. These pages set up the background for the Jamestown colony. Study the timeline on pages 2-3.

> **Note:** Genevieve Foster's "World" books provide a wealth of information about the history of North America as well as the world. This study focuses on the content relevant to the history of the United States. Therefore, sections of these books will be skipped in the reading assignments. If desired, refer to the charts on pages 102-108 of this guide for guidance on using Foster's books to incorporate world history.

3. To learn more about Sir Francis Drake, visit: pbslearningmedia.org/resource/pbs-world-explorers-francis-drake/.

4. Create a new section in the portfolio titled: Colonization in America: Jamestown.

LESSON 10

1. Read pages 39-40, 52-54, 65-68, and 85-90 of *The World of Capt. John Smith*.

2. Introduce *Pocahontas* by Joseph Bruchac. Bruchac (a Nulhegan Abenaki citizen) states that one of the wisest things Native Elders taught him was that all humans have two ears because our creator wished us to remember two sides of a story. This book provides the benefit of seeing the perspectives of both the Powhatan people and the Jamestown settlers. As you read through this book, note how key events were viewed differently by each group. Read the background information on pages 167-173 for context. You may also want to review the notes on historic language on pages 153-166 and tab the glossaries for easy reference. Next, read the Preface and Chapters 1-4. Discussion and narration prompts:

> Discuss the idea of culture and possible definitions before looking it up in the dictionary. Who or what is culture? What are the characteristics of culture? Compare the definition you formed through discussion to the dictionary definition.

> The Powhatan passed down an oral history through storytelling. The English recorded their stories in the written word. Both methods are time-honored ways of recording history. Compare the two methods. Discuss how oral history differs from written history. To what degree is it the same?

> Narrate the first conflict between the Powhatan and the English from both perspectives. Discuss how looking at it from both sides expands your understanding of the event.

3. Using the map at the beginning of *Pocahontas*, mark the following on the map of North America.

    Rappahannock   Werowocomoco   Powhatan

LESSON 11

1. Read pages 124-125, 136-142, and 150-153 of *The World of Capt. John Smith*.

2. Read Chapters 5-8 of *Pocahontas*. Discussion and narration prompts:

> In *Peacemaker,* we examined the importance of storytelling. Now discuss how the Powhatan and English tell stories. How do Smith's stories fill in the details of his life and tell us about him as a person? Do Pocahontas's stories accomplish the same purpose? How are their stories similar or different?

> Chapters 7 and 8 provide two perspectives on the same incident. Compare these perspectives and where the communication broke down.

3. The following videos outline the difficulties and cultural barriers between the Powhatan and the English. Find both on the Fairfax Network – Fairfax County Public Schools YouTube channel:

> "Virginia's First People: The Powhatan—The Culture Barrier"
> "The Language Barrier: Powhatan vs. English"

4. Begin working on a project from the "Activities and Handicraft" section.

LESSON 12

1. As John Smith was adventuring and England was getting used to King James, a group of English Separatists was growing increasingly frustrated with the state of religion in England. Read about the Separatists and Pilgrims on pages 166-169 and 173-176 of *The World of Capt. John Smith*. We will be reading more about the Pilgrims following our study of Jamestown

2. Read Chapters 9-13 of *Pocahontas*. Discussion and narration prompts:

> Pocahontas was curious and asked many questions. Relate how Pocahontas's questioning nature helped her to see the possibility of peace between the Powhatan and the English. How can curiosity increase understanding? How can asking good questions make one more aware and lead to wisdom?

> There have been several conflicts between the Powhatan and the English in the story. Has reading about these conflicts from the differing perspectives of Pocahontas and Smith affected your understanding of these historic disagreements? Discuss how misunderstanding and assumption contributed to the disputes.

> How was the English class system enforced in Jamestown? Did this old and entrenched social system work in the new world? Why or why not?

3. Continue working on your handicraft project or choose another to complete.

1. Sculpture of Chief Wahunsonacock, leader of the Powhatan people 2. John Smith, c. 1616
3. Artist's conception of aerial view of Jamestown, Virginia in 1614

LESSON 13

1. Read pages 177-198 of *The World of Capt. John Smith* to learn about French, Spanish, and English efforts in America.

2. Mark the following on the map of North America:

St. Augustine, FL   Santa Fe, NM   Grand Canyon
Rio Grande River   El Paso, TX

3. Read Chapters 14-18 of *Pocahontas*. Discussion and narration prompts:

Throughout *Pocahontas*, you have read about many pivotal moments when history could have been affected if leaders had chosen a different path. Choose one of these crucial moments and analyze it. In your notebook, make two columns: Pros and Cons. Write at least five benefits and drawbacks for each option. Once you've evaluated the decision, determine how you would have handled the situation, and create an argument defending your position. How does hindsight make your decision more straightforward than it was for the people living in 1607?

Example: Should the Jamestown president give the sick people in Jamestown more food or continue to distribute it equally among the community?

Pros:
- It will help them heal
- It is kind
- It is hospitable
- It is not greedy
- It might be the right thing to do
- They may have more able men to save the colony

Cons:
- They could run out of food
- The sick could be pretending
- They would all starve faster
- They might die anyway
- It's one way to get rid of a bad guy
- It gives more power to the president

LESSON 14

1. Read pages 199-222 of *The World of Capt. John Smith*. **Parental Warning:** Page 203 includes the word squaw. This word, while once widely used to refer to Native women, is considered offensive by Native peoples.

2. Using the map on page 203 of *The World of Capt. John Smith*, mark the following territories on the map of North America:

Algonquin territory   Iroquois territory   Cherokee territory
Creek territory   Seminole territory   Ute territory
Pueblo territory   Navaho territory   Aztec territory

Note: These were the largest and most powerful tribes and nations at the time of early English, Spanish, and French colonialization, and this map does not represent smaller or individual tribes.

For more detailed information, see the map on page 15 of this guide and visit: www.npr.org/sections/codeswitch/2014/06/24/323665644/the-map-of-native-american-tribes-youve-never-seen-before

LESSON 14 continued

3. Read Chapters 19-23 of *Pocahontas*. Discussion and narration prompt:

> The Powhatan tribe gave Pocahontas many names, and they named John Smith the Little Red-Haired Warrior. Naming things is a meaningful gift that God has given his image-bearers. Create an honorable nickname for a friend, family member, or pet that describes their character. Do this activity with your whole family or class, with each member bestowing descriptive and complimentary names on one another.

4. Create a *pawcoransak*, or a remembering stone, for your family. Many cultures, like the Powhatan, have used stones or monuments to record history, mark significant events, or remind people of essential truths. First, choose an important story, family value, or a meaningful word, phrase, quote, or verse you want to memorialize. Choose a stone and decorate it using paint or paint pens. Inscribe it with the words or symbols. Place the stone in a special spot.

LESSON 15

1. Finish reading *Pocahontas*. Discussion and narration prompts:

> John Smith led an expedition to hunt and trade and, in the course of the journey, lost men and was captured. Why did the Powhatan warriors spare Smith's life? Discuss how Smith's courage influenced the Powhatan. In what ways did this interaction surprise you?

> Describe what happened when Pocahontas finally met John Smith. How did Pocahontas show hospitality to John Smith?

2. Over the next few days, write a treaty between the Powhatan and the English. Given the benefit of hindsight, what provisions would you include if you were able to travel back in time and advise both parties? Be sure to have regulations for land use and ownership, hunting and planting rights, procedures to settle disputes, along with governance and enforcement of the agreement.

3. Archaeologists found Werowocomoco in 2001. Long thought to be lost to history, the discovery was an exciting and meaningful event in Native and American historical research. Check it out here:
www.nps.gov/cajo/planyourvisit/werowocomoco.htm

LESSON 16

1. Read pages 223-242 and 254-259 of *The World of Capt. John Smith*.

2. We will now turn our attention to Leyden, Holland, and read about the English Separatists we know as the Pilgrims. Begin *Almost Home* by Wendy Lawton. Read Chapters 1-3. Note: Italicized words are defined in the glossary at the back of *Almost Home* beginning on page 141. If desired, record any unfamiliar words and their definitions in your notebook.

This lesson is continued on page 31.

The Mayflower, artist unknown

LESSON 16 continued

Discussion and narration prompts:

The Pilgrims enjoyed religious freedom in Leyden but faced cultural challenges. Describe these social obstacles.

Describe the Pilgrims' frustrations and criticisms of the Church of England.

Consider the sacrifices the Pilgrims made to worship according to their convictions. If faced with similar circumstances, which losses would you find most challenging? Can you empathize with Mary's desire for belonging and stability?

The community shared by the Pilgrims created solid bonds and provided comfort as they left their homes and friends. Consider how this community was built. How did Mary seek ways to support her fellow Pilgrims? How did she draw strength from her community?

3. Create a new section in the portfolio titled "The Pilgrims of Plymouth."

4. To learn more about Bradford and Brewster, watch "Virtual Voyages: The homes of Bradford and Brewster" on the Mayflower 400 UK YouTube channel. Also, visit the following site to learn more about the Pilgrims' time in Leyden (now spelled Leiden): www.mayflower400leiden.com/

LESSON 17

1. Read pages 254-259 and 269-273 of *The World of Capt. John Smith*.

2. Read Chapters 4-6 of *Almost Home*. Discussion and narration prompt:

Why were the delays in setting sail so worrisome? If you have familiarity with the Pilgrims' story, you already know that their first year in New England was devastating. Given this knowledge, consider the options available to the Pilgrims. What would you have done if you were on the *Speedwell* and had to turn back? Would you have stayed in England or continued on the *Mayflower*? Why?

3. Read more about the harrowing voyage from Plymouth to Cape Cod:
   www.history.com/news/mayflower-journey-pilgrims-america.

LESSON 18

1. Read pages 278-296 of *The World of Capt. John Smith*.

2. Read Chapters 7-9 of *Almost Home*. Learn more:

The Mayflower Compact is one of the foundational documents of our nation's history. Visit the following link to understand how it helped establish government by consent, freedom of religion, and other essential liberties we still enjoy today:
www.crf-usa.org/foundations-of-our-constitution/mayflower-compact.html

3. Mark the following on the map of North America:

Cape Cod   Cape Cod Bay   Provincetown, MA
Plymouth, MA

LESSON 19

1. Read pages 297-315 of *The World of Capt. John Smith*.

2. Read Chapters 10-12 and the Epilogue of *Almost Home*. Discussion and narration prompts:

> On page 128, Mary heard Samoset relate the story of the great plague that wiped out the people who lived at Patuxet. Describe Mary's reaction to this story. Discuss the idea, held by some, that the plague was a providential event to pave the way for the Pilgrims' settlement.

> Discuss the concept of home and Mary's evolving understanding of this idea. Describe the impact her faith has on her thoughts about home.

3. We have seen how vital the Mayflower Compact was to establishing religious freedoms and self-government, but it also helped establish a tradition of philanthropy! Check it out here:
www.learningtogive.org/resources/mayflower-compact.

LESSON 20

1. In *Almost Home,* we read the Pilgrims' story from their perspective. We saw how faith motivated their actions and sacrifices, and we followed their journey to the new world. In both *Almost Home* and *The World of Capt. John Smith*, we see these events from the European perspective. We will now turn to Wampanoag voices to look at these events from their point of view. Together, this creates a more complete picture of this important period in American history. Read the following articles:

> www.smithsonianmag.com/blogs/national-museum-american-indian/2017/11/23/everyones-history-matters-and-wampanoag-indian-thanksgiving-story-deserves-be-known/

> https://indiancountrytoday.com/archive/the-wampanoag-side-of-the-first-thanksgiving-story

2. The Pilgrims' treaty with the Wampanoag resulted in 50 years of peace. During those 50 years, more and more English settlers came to New England. Their demand for land and poor treatment of the Native tribes finally erupted into war. Massasoit's grandson, Metacom (called Philip by the English), came to a point where he felt that he could no longer ignore the abuses of the English. The following has been attributed to him:

> Brothers, you see this vast country before us, which the Great Spirit gave to our fathers and us; you see the buffalo and deer that now are our support. Brothers, you see these little ones, our wives and children, who are looking to us for food and raiment; and you now see the foe before you, that they have grown insolent and bold; that all our ancient customs are disregarded; the treaties made by our fathers and us are broken, and all of us insulted; our council fires disregarded, and all the ancient customs of our fathers; our brothers murdered before our eyes, and their spirits cry to us for revenge. Brothers, these people from the unknown world will cut down our groves, spoil our hunting and planting grounds, and drive us and our children from the graves of our fathers, and our council fires, and enslave our women and children.
> Source: http://voicesofdemocracy.umd.edu/apess-eulogy-speech-text/

In 1675, the peace between the Wampanoag and the English came to an end with King Philip's War. Research this war and record your findings in the portfolio.

1. *Pilgrims Going To Church* by George Henry Boughton, 1867
2. Recreation of Plimoth Plantation in Plymouth, Massachusetts

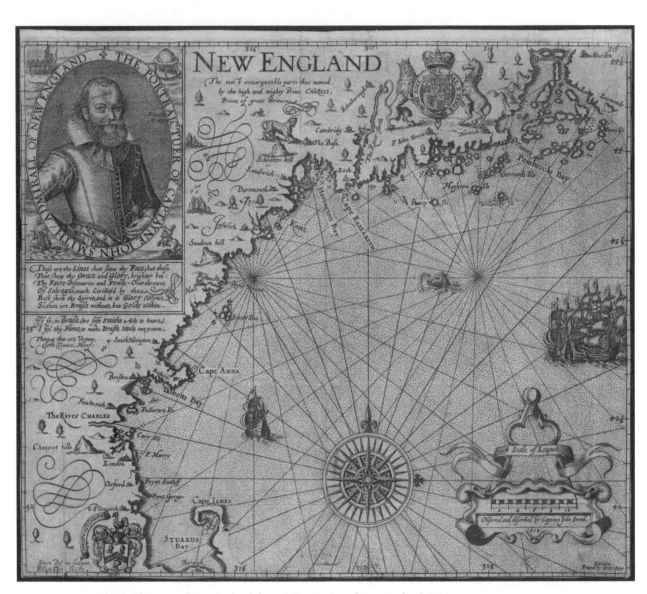

John Smith's map of New England, from *A Description of New England*, 1616.

LESSON 21

1. Read pages 321-325, 343-346, 363-371, and 384-400 of *The World of Capt. John Smith*. The English colonies in Virginia and New England were well-established when John Smith died in England in 1631. They continued to grow, and energetic and bustling cities emerged throughout New England.

2. Mark the following on the map of North America:

Boston, MA   Salem, MA   New Amsterdam (New York)
Charlestown, MA

3. In the United States, the actions of the past are still disputed today. Read the following article and then research the conflict to build a case supporting either the Wampanoag or the Narragansett Improvement Company. How will you address the concerns of the opposing party? How does your historical knowledge inform your position?

www.reuters.com/article/us-usa-indians-rhodeisland/piles-of-rocks-spark-an-american-indian-mystery-idUSN1625947520070518

LESSON 22

1. Despite both being English colonies, Massachusetts and Virginia were very different, and these differences would shape the future United States and eventually lead to Civil War. The following videos will help explain these differences while also providing a review of what we have covered so far. Find them at khanacademy.org.

"Society and religion in the New England colonies"
"Politics and native relations in the New England colonies"
"The Middle colonies"
"Developing an American colonial identity"

2. The Pilgrims sought a place where they could worship freely and maintain their identity as Englishmen. This pursuit would later inspire the guaranteed right to worship freely that we enjoy today. Despite this, many of the later colonists, particularly the Puritans, failed to extend religious freedom to other Christian sects, and religious conflict plagued New England in its early years. Choose one person or event from the following list to research. Record your findings in the portfolio.

Roger Williams
Anne Hutchinson
Mary Dyer
The Salem Witch Trials

PART III

The Later Colonial Period and the French & Indian War

1706–1776

Penn's Treaty with the Indians by Edward Hicks, c. 1830

*T*he young colonies survived and entered a period of rapid growth and expansion. Soon Massachusetts and Virginia were joined by New Hampshire, Connecticut, Rhode Island, Delaware, New York, New Jersey, Pennsylvania, Maryland, North Carolina, South Carolina, and Georgia. From 1625 to 1775, the population in these colonies grew from 2000 to 2.4 million people.

Colonial expansion put intense pressure on the tribes and nations whose land the settlers claimed for themselves, either through treaty or by force. This would lead to the French and Indian War, which set the stage for the Revolutionary War.

The colonies were governed by a system known as mercantilism. Merchants and business owners in the colonies were only permitted to trade with England. This ensured that wealth primarily flowed from America to England.

Slavery was legal in all 13 colonies and was integral to mercantilism. Traders bought enslaved Africans and brought them to the Americas, where they were traded for raw goods like cotton, lumber, furs, and food crops, which were then taken to England. These materials were then manufactured and exported as finished goods like furniture, guns, and cloth back to the colonies as well as to East Africa, where they were exchanged for enslaved laborers.

In this section, we will be reading about colonial life, the experience of an enslaved African prince, the lives of the founding fathers, and the rising cry for freedom in America. We will move back and forth a bit as some of the literature moves into the Revolutionary War period, but that will simply introduce our in-depth study of that topic later.

Rabbit Trails //

A Voice of Her Own: The Story of Phillis Wheatley, Slave Poet
by Kathryn Lasky, illustrated by Paul Lee
This is an engaging biography of Phillis Wheatley, demonstrating the young girl's incredible intellect and deep sense of justice and dignity, even when those around her questioned her abilities.

Chains by Laurie Halse Anderson
This heart-wrenching novel captures the pain and indignities experienced by enslaved people in the colonies. Isabel and her sister, Ruth, had been promised their freedom, but their master's death brings a cruel twist of fate. Suddenly, Isabel finds herself in a precarious position with an opportunity to spy on her loyalist masters and possibly attain freedom.
Parental Warning: This book contains instances of cruelty and domestic violence.

Colonial Living by Edwin Tunis
This title is a vigorous re-creation of 17th- and 18th-century America and of the everyday living of those sturdy men and women who carved a way of life out of the wilderness, from the first Native settlers to those English and Dutch adventurers and colonists.

Character Connection //

PERSEVERANCE: Perseverance is continuous effort and determination despite difficulties and setbacks. Discuss this virtue and how one cultivates it. As you read through the literature in this section, discuss who demonstrated perseverance. Which characters did not? How does perseverance help the character endure hard times? Discuss the meaning of perseverance as it pertains to these verses.

1 Chronicles 16:11
Romans 5:3-5
Romans 12:12
Galatians 6:9
Hebrews 12:1
Hebrews 10:36
James 1:2-4

Poems on Various Subjects, Religious and Moral: By an African American Slave Woman, Writing in the 18th Century
by Phillis Wheatley
Wheatley's voice and poetic genius helped shape American literature and are an essential part of any home library.

The Trials of Phillis Wheatley: America's First Black Poet and Her Encounters with the Founding Fathers
by Henry Louis Gates, Jr.
Rich in historical detail and biographical information, Gates expounds on the legacy of Wheatley as well as the effect of Jefferson's refusal to acknowledge Wheatley's genius.

To Be a Slave by Julius Lester
This Newbery Honor book preserves the words of enslaved people, providing first-person accounts of the indignities, abuses, and horrors of slavery. This is an essential historical document recording the dehumanizing effects of slavery, both on the enslaved and the enslaver. **Parental Warning:** The content is offensive, violent, and necessary for gaining an understanding of the realities of slavery.

The Amazing Life of Benjamin Franklin by James Giblin, illustrated by Michael Dooling
Get to know this fascinating founding father through the engaging text and beautiful illustrations in this easy-to-read biography.

Creative Writing Prompt //

In this section, you will be reading the autobiography of Olaudah Equiano, who wrote his story because he believed that every event in a person's life deserves to be examined for the purpose of learning. Choose an event from your life and write about it and what you learned through the experience.

Activities & Handicraft //

Benjamin Franklin

STAMP ACT: Research the Stamp Act and re-create some of the stamps using construction paper, paints, markers, etc. Add to the portfolio.

TAXATION: The colonists' fury at being taxed by Parliament, where they had no representation, was a touchpoint for the revolutionary movement. We now pay much higher taxes than the colonists paid, but the rates are passed by our local, state, and federal governing bodies. Research how taxes are enacted and the taxes your family pays (i.e., sales tax, income tax, property tax, etc.). Next, research what taxes pay for in your community.

CROSS-STITCH & EMBROIDERY: The American colonists produced exquisite works of tapestry, cross-stitch, and embroidery. Read all about them, and view some amazing samples at the following link:

> www.metmuseum.org/toah/hd/need/hd_need.htm

Whether you're an experienced stitcher or you want to try your hand for the first time, you can find many instructional videos available online to help you gather materials and get started. Here's a great collection of free pattern downloads to help you get started:

> www.thesprucecrafts.com/top-free-embroidery-designs-4157614

DYEING CLOTH THE COLONIAL WAY: Colonists who boycotted British goods adapted by making their own cloth dyes out of nuts, herbs, roots, and plants. Learn more and dye your own cloth here:

> www.tinasdynamichomeschoolplus.com/cloth-dyeing

Online Resources //

LIBERTY'S KIDS
> This dramatic animated series is a fun way to learn about the American Revolution. All episodes from the series are available for free on the Liberty's Kids – WildBrain YouTube channel.

HISTORIC BOSTON
> Boston is one of our most historic cities and has grown and changed dramatically from when Benjamin Franklin was born. Visit the following site to do an activity comparing Boston in 1722 with the city today:
> www.nationalgeographic.org/activity/comparing-historical-maps/

TRIANGULAR TRADE
> The Huntington Museum has produced a detailed unit on the Triangular Trade that brought enslaved people to the Americas and took raw goods from the colonies to their ruling nations. For anyone wanting to do a deep dive, this is a helpful resource:
> www.huntington.org/sites/default/files/pdfs/lhthtriangulartrade.pdf

COLONIAL WILLIAMSBURG
> The living museum at Williamsburg, Virginia, offers a wealth of its resources online including lectures, how-tos, instructional videos, and much more:
> www.colonialwilliamsburg.org/

Research Essays & Projects //

SLAVERY

Write an essay answering the question that was beginning to circulate in England and the colonies, "Is slavery immoral?" Support your argument with primary sources and quotes from enslaved people. Consider the fact that Equiano considered Mr. King to be a "good" master. Is it possible to enslave people and be good?

THE POWER OF WORDS & BIAS

Early in his life, Benjamin Franklin recognized that using and understanding words effectively was a powerful force. To see this idea in action, choose a recent news story that interests you. Next, visit allsides.com and read articles about your chosen topic from across the political spectrum: liberal to conservative. Consider how these articles present the topic. We all bring assumptions and biases to our reading, no matter what the subject. Consider which articles you agree with the most and which challenge your beliefs or assumptions. What does that reveal about your bias on this topic? What words jump out to you? Did reading a variety of opinions affect your original position or opinion? How were words used to convey and influence opinion?

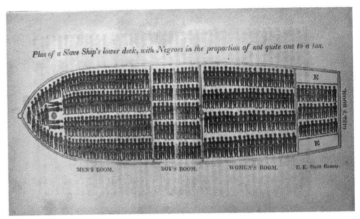

Diagram of a slave ship

FREEDOM OF THE PRESS

"In the conduct of my newspaper I carefully excluded all libeling and personal abuse which is of late years become so disgraceful to our country." Consider Franklin's standard for the material he would print in his newspaper. Read the First Amendment to the U.S. Constitution. Research the controversy over social media platforms limiting the information they allow to be shared. Could Franklin's guidance be applied to this controversy? What role, if any, could the federal government have in ensuring freedom of speech? Are libel and slander protected under the First Amendment?

TAX EVASION

The Penn family held the royal charter for the Pennsylvania colony. During Franklin's life, the Penns, living in England, were notorious for raising taxes on the colony's citizens while exempting their personal holdings and businesses from those taxes. As Franklin wrote: "These public quarrels were all at bottom owning to the proprietaries, our hereditary governors, who, when any expense was to be incurred for the defense of their province, with incredible meanness instructed their deputies to pass no act for levying the necessary taxes unless their vast estates were in the same act expressly excused; and they had ever taken bonds of these deputies to obey such instructions." In 2021, an investigation of IRS documents revealed that top-earning Americans paid the lowest federal income taxes and sometimes paid nothing at all. Write a paper comparing this revelation with the Penns' policy of exempting themselves from English taxes. Are there similarities or critical differences? Do you think it is fair to draw parallels between the Penns and Elon Musk or Jeff Bezos? The following is a link to the 2021 report:

> www.propublica.org/article/the-secret-irs-files-trove-of-never-before-seen-records-reveal-how-the-wealthiest-avoid-income-tax

PROTEST & CIVIL UNREST

Dr. Martin Luther King, Jr., once wrote that "a riot is the language of the unheard." The United States has a long history of political protest and rioting stretching back to its colonial days. How did protest and rioting give the colonists a way to express their sense of injustice and injury? Write a paper comparing a current or recent protest or riot with one from the colonial period. The following link provides a list of incidents of civil unrest in colonial America: https://en.wikipedia.org/wiki/List_of_incidents_of_civil_unrest_in_Colonial_North_America

LESSON 23

1. Introduce *The Kidnapped Prince* by Olaudah Equiano. Equiano was born in the mid-18th century, so his story takes place when the colonies were becoming increasingly unhappy with English rule. Against this backdrop, it is essential to understand the enslaved experience. Equiano's life is truly remarkable; he fought in the French and Indian War, earned his freedom, overcame incredible hardship and challenges, and wrote his autobiography "to serve the interests of humanity." Read the Introduction, About this Adaptation, and the Prologue on pages vii-1. Discussion prompt:

> Equiano wrote: "I think no event is really important unless we use it to become better and wiser. To people who think about their lives, almost everything that happens or that they read, provides a way of learning. To those who don't examine their lives, all the experience of the ages is worthless." Discuss this idea and how it relates to the study of history. How can you honor Equiano's labor in telling his story?

2. Create a new section in the portfolio titled "Olaudah Equiano." Add the quote directly above to this new section.

3. Watch "The Transatlantic Slave Trade: CrashCourse Black American History #1" on the CrashCourse YouTube channel. **Parental Warning:** This video introduces challenging subjects, including sexual violence, torture, suicide, and more. Knowledge of these horrors is essential to understanding slavery. The video also contains mild, historically accurate nudity.

// To pronounce Equiano's name correctly, watch "Olaudah Equiano | Black History Month for Kids" on the Little Crowns TV YouTube Channel. Other videos have pronunciations that are heavily anglicized and, therefore, not accurate.

LESSON 24

1. Read pages 3-35 of *The Kidnapped Prince*. Narration and discussion prompts:

> Describe Equiano's home and native culture. Did any aspect of his life before enslavement surprise you? Why? Compare the life he expected to have with the one he experienced following his capture and enslavement.

> Equiano wrote: "…I felt a little less scared, knowing they were taking us to work. If that was all they did to me, I could stand it." Discuss how slavery was not merely "work." Consider how the enslaved were brutalized, torn from their families, and dehumanized.

2. Listen to a narration of Equiano's work by watching "Olaudah Equiano" on the cconno89 YouTube channel.

3. Trace the map on pages 139-140 of *The Kidnapped Prince* and label it "The Travels of Olaudah Equiano, 1755-1767." Add the map to the portfolio.

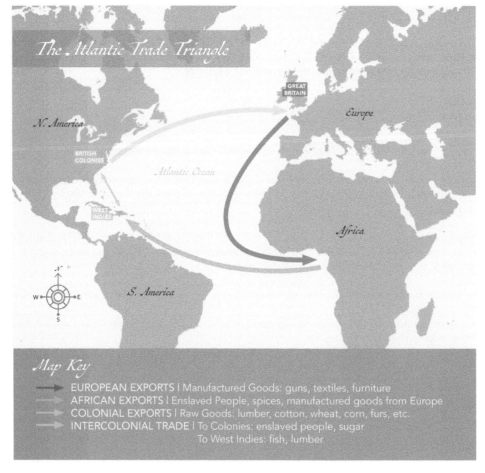

1. Frontispiece from 1789 edition of *The Interesting Narrative of the Life of Olaudah Equiano, Or Gustavus Vassa, The African* 2. Poem included in a later edition of Equiano's autobiography 3. The Atlantic Trade Triangle by Ryan Maloney

LESSON 25

1. Read pages 36-62 of *The Kidnapped Prince*. Note: A grampus is a type of dolphin. Narration and discussion prompts:

> Equiano observed that slavery was dehumanizing to both the enslaved and the enslaver. Discuss this and provide examples from your reading.
>
> Equiano was dropped into a world where he knew nothing about the customs, language, or people. Try to imagine what that would be like. Consider how his young mind tried to use ideas from his childhood to explain things in his new life. Have you had an experience where you were utterly confused by everything? How did your mind try to figure out what was going on?

2. Captain Pascal was reluctant to allow Equiano's baptism. Read the following article about the history of missionary efforts in Africa and how some considered baptism a threat to the institution of slavery:
> https://calendar.eji.org/racial-injustice/sep/23

3. Choose a research topic from page 40 and begin looking for source material and formulating your thesis statement.

LESSON 26

1. Read pages 63-83 of *The Kidnapped Prince*. **Parental Warning**: These pages portray some of the brutal realities of slavery. Discussion and narration prompts:

> Equiano states that Captain Pascal taught him morals and honesty by saying, "God would not love" Equiano if he lied or disobeyed. Consider how this gave Pascal even more control over Equiano. How could James 3:1 be applied to this situation? How did Pascal shape Equiano's view of God in untrue ways?
>
> The relationship between slavery and Christianity was fraught with conflict, hypocrisy, and sin. Discuss Equiano's conversation with Mr. D– regarding the conflict between the principles of Christianity and the practice of slavery.

2. Visit the following website to learn more about the publication and illustrations in Equiano's autobiography:
> https://graphicarts.princeton.edu/2016/03/22/olaudah-equiano/

3. Draw your own version of the map to the left and add it to the portfolio. Label it "The Atlantic Trade Triangle."

1. Engraving from Voltaire's *Candide*: Depicts the scene where Candide and Cacambo meet a maimed slave of a sugar mill near Surinam. Its caption reads in English, "It is at this price that you eat sugar in Europe"; a line said by the enslaved man in the text. The man has had his hand cut off for getting a finger stuck in a millstone and his leg removed for trying to run away.
2. Image from *Ten Views in the Island of Antigua* depicting the digging of holes in the cane fields by enslaved laborers. Images by William Clark, c. 1823.

LESSON 27

1. Read pages 84-111 of *The Kidnapped Prince*. Discussion prompts:

> Equiano saw and experienced great injustices and violent crimes perpetrated against enslaved people in the West Indies. Even though Christians committed many of these horrors, Equiano's faith gave him comfort and strength. How do you think Equiano was able to separate his faith from the actions of self-proclaimed Christians? How did Equiano experience God's love and provision?

> Discuss Equiano's understanding of honor. How did his commitment to honesty guide his actions? What did it cost him?

> Discuss Equiano's assertion that "cowardice is always the companion of cruelty."

2. Describe the state of a free or enslaved Black man in the West Indies. Write down this description. Be sure to include the fact that free and enslaved Blacks had no legal avenues to pursue justice, were unable to appeal to the law, were given much more severe sentences than white people for the same crimes, and lived in a constant state of fear. Add this description to your portfolio. While the description given by Equiano refers to the West Indies, the same injustices were rampant in the English colonies and would worsen following the Revolutionary War. We will learn more about this later in our study.

3. To learn more about Equiano, visit https://equiano.uk/.

LESSON 28

1. Finish reading *The Kidnapped Prince*.

2. Write a biography of Equiano's life, including the aspects you found most remarkable. Add to the portfolio. Illustrate with drawings or printed images.

3. One of the great Christian hymns, *Amazing Grace*, was written by a former slave ship captain, John Newton. Learn more by watching "Amazing Grace: The Story Behind the Song" on the Oxvision Films YouTube channel.

1. *Benjamin Franklin*, artist unknown. 2. Sculpture of Benjamin Franklin in Boston, 1856

VOCABULARY //

James Daugherty uses some advanced vocabulary in *Poor Richard*. Define any of the following terms you are not familiar with in preparation for your reading.

doggerel (13)	tallow (14)	rout (20)	genial (20)
satire (21)	epistle (21)	jibe (22)	sloop (23)
stevedores (25)	succumbed (26)	abate (28)	fagged (28)
indentured (28)	itinerant (28)	burnished (29)	coquetry (31)
dullard (36)	revel (38)	swagger (38)	nonchalant (38)
vulgarity (38)	reconcile (38)	wistful (39)	lampooning (39)
libel (39)	ovation (40)	munificent (40)	morose (41)
steerage (42)	debonair (43)	lackeys (46)	carouse (46)
lurid (46)	lure (46)	bawdy (46)	ambrosia (46)
ferret (verb 47)	cockney (47)	banter (47)	imprudent (48)
novelties (48)	descry (49)	suffusion (49)	card sharp (53)
yokels (51)	drollery (52)	anecdotes (52)	brooding (53)
lingo (55)	trundling (58)	decorous (61)	prognostication (61)
venerable (61)	hodgepodge (61)	inculcate (63)	benignity (63)
luminous (65)	ague (69)	dither (75)	indemnities (75)
infallible (76)	invincible (76)	vehemence (76)	exorbitant (77)
exuberant (77)			

LESSON 29

1. We will now turn our attention to Boston and a man whose life's work shaped much of our understanding of what it means to be an American: Benjamin Franklin. Begin *Poor Richard* by James Daugherty by reading the inscription on page 7. This message encapsulates one of the great reasons to study history. Write it out in the portfolio along with your thoughts about it. Begin a new section in your notebook titled "Benjamin Franklin."

2. Mark the following on the map of North America:

New Jersey   Perth Amboy, NJ   Burlington, PA
Philadelphia, PA

3. Read pages 10-31 of *Poor Richard*. Discussion prompt:

Discuss Franklin's response to Plato: "I was charmed with it, adopted it, dropped my abrupt contradictions and positive argumentation, and put on the humble inquirer."

LESSON 30

1. Read pages 32-55 of *Poor Richard*. **Note:** This book perpetuates the rumor that King George did not speak English. While this may have been true at the beginning of his reign, George quickly learned the language, as evidenced by court documents. Discussion and narration prompts:

Page 41: Describe how Franklin's thinking changed as he began to see and experience the ripple effect of people's personal decisions.

Consider Franklin's list of virtues. Do you think his list stands the test of time and remains relevant today? What, if any, virtues would you add or remove?

This book presents King George with a distinctly negative bias. Pick out some words or phrases used to describe King George in *Poor Richard* that reveal this bias. Research George's life and determine if Daugherty's portrayal is entirely accurate. Record findings in the portfolio.

2. Choose a research topic from page 40, and begin researching and preparing a rough draft.

LESSON 31

1. Throughout this section, we will be reading *George Washington's World*, both to provide context for the other literature and to learn about the lives of our first president and other key figures of the American Revolution. Read pages ix-27.

2. Read pages 56-83 of *Poor Richard*. **Parental Warning:** These chapters contain offensive terms to refer to Native Americans. Discussion and research prompts:

Benjamin Franklin bought, sold, and utilized enslaved people. Are you surprised to learn this? Why? Research Franklin's thoughts of slavery and how they changed over time. The following resource is helpful: www.pbs.org/benfranklin/l3_citizen_abolitionist.html

These chapters refer to the Six Nations. This is the Iroquois League of Peace we read about in *Peacemaker*. At the time of its founding, it was a league of five nations. Research the sixth nation and how it came to join the Iroquois Confederacy. Record your findings in the portfolio.

3. Watch "The French and Indian War as a Turning Point (APUSH Period 3)" on the Tom Richey YouTube channel.

LESSON 32

1. Read pages 56-62 and 73-82 of *George Washington's World*.

2. The following article by Ross Douthat explains the importance of the French and Indian War and contains a discourse on the roles of patriotism and skepticism in studying history:

www.nytimes.com/2021/07/13/opinion/french-indian-war-american-history.html

LESSON 33

1. Read pages 84-101 of *Poor Richard*. Discussion prompts:

Discuss Edmund Burke's statement on the English colonists' love of freedom and right to representation in the English constitution:

"The temper and character which prevail in our Colonies are, I am afraid, unalterable by any human art. We cannot, I fear, alter the pedigree of this fierce people and persuade them that they are not sprung from a nation in whose veins the blood of freedom circulates. The language in which they would hear you tell them this tale would detect the imposition; your speech would betray you. An Englishman is the unfittest person on earth to argue another Englishman into slavery.
"The question with me is not whether you have a right to render your people miserable, but whether it is not your interest to make them happy. It is not what a lawyer tells me I may do, but what humanity, reason, and justice tell me I ought to do. My idea, therefore, without considering whether we yield as a matter of right, or grant as a matter of favor, is to admit the people of our Colonies into an interest in the constitution."

2. Read pages 83-101 of *George Washington's World*. Discussion and research prompts:

Discuss Pontiac's war against the British, and consider both sides. Once you have evaluated the Ottawa and English perspectives, determine which side you believe to be more morally justified. Explain why.

General Amherst's plan to spread smallpox among the Indian tribes was biological warfare, but recent research questions the strategy's effectiveness. Read the following article to learn more:

https://www.history.com/news/colonists-native-americans-smallpox-blankets

3. Write a brief report on the French and Indian War, tracing its role in leading to the American Revolutionary War. Add to the portfolio.

LESSON 34

1. In the last lesson, you read about Phillis Wheatley, the first black woman poet to be published in the United States. Phillis's life was a testimony to her stunning intellect, sharp wit, and keen skills of observation and criticism. Create a new section in the portfolio titled "Phillis Wheatley, American Poet." Learn more about her at the following resources:

"Phillis Wheatley: The First Published African-American Poet | Black Patriots | History" on the History YouTube channel.

"Phillis Wheatley: CrashCourse Black American History #7" on the CrashCourse YouTube channel

2. Read the following poem by Wheatley:

"On Being Brought from Africa to America"

'Twas mercy brought me from my Pagan land,
Taught my benighted soul to understand
That there's a God, that there's a Saviour too:
Once I redemption neither sought nor knew.
Some view our sable race with scornful eye,
"Their colour is a diabolic die."
Remember, Christians, Negros, black as Cain,
May be refin'd, and join th' angelic train.

Reread the poem a few times and write down your thoughts. Next, watch the following videos for literary analysis:

"Phillis Wheatley's 'On Being Brought from Africa to America' Read by Cornelius Eady" on the Tate Street YouTube channel

"Analyzing Phillis Wheatley's 'On Being Brought From Africa to America'" on the Tammie Pierce YouTube channel

3. Read several of Wheatley's poems online at the following link, and write out your favorite. Add to the portfolio along with a brief report on her life.

www.poetryfoundation.org/poets/phillis-wheatley

Frontispiece from *Poems on Various Subjects, Religious and Moral* by Phillis Wheatley

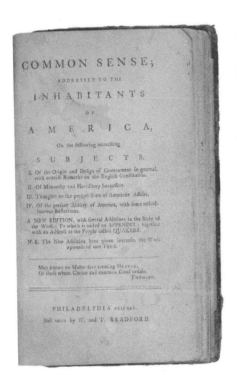

1. Frontispiece of *Common Sense*, 1776 2. *Thomas Paine* by Laurent Dabos, 1791

LESSON 35

1. Create a new section in the portfolio titled "Lead-Up to Revolution."

2. Read pages 111-118 and 122-129 of *George Washington's World*. Discussion and narration prompts:

> Write out a list of the colonists' grievances against England. Record in the portfolio.

> Describe the "tea trick." How was this supposed to legitimize the English taxation of tea? Did it work? See page 128.

3. Benjamin Franklin had no way of knowing that his introduction of Thomas Paine to the colonies would strike the match that would light the fire of revolution. Learn more about Paine and his *Common Sense* at the following:

> "History Brief: Thomas Paine's Common Sense" on the Reading Through History YouTube channel

> "Liberty's Kids 112 - Common Sense with Thomas Paine | History Cartoons for Children" on the Liberty's Kids – WildBrain YouTube channel

> www.history.com/news/thomas-paine-common-sense-revolution

LESSON 36

1. Read pages 136-139 and 154-180 of *George Washington's World*.

2. Read pages 102-109 of *Poor Richard*.

3. To prepare for our next section, review the following article:

> www.history.com/news/american-revolution-causes

4. To conclude this section, make Patriot's Tea. Express your support for the rebel's cause by making tea in the colonial tradition. Visit the following links for inspiration:

> www.bostonteapartyship.com/tea-blog/liberty-teas-of-colonial-boston

> www.bostonteapartyship.com/liberty-teas

PART IV

The Revolutionary War
1776–1783

Passage of the Delaware by Thomas Sully, c. 1819

By early 1776, many colonists had reached a breaking point. What had begun as murmurs of discontent and whisperings of frustration bloomed into outright rebellion as the colonists resisted the heavy thumb of Parliament and King George. Thomas Paine's *Common Sense* gave words to the frustrations and injustices felt by the Americans. Mercantilism continued to transfer wealth from America to England, and the colonies had no representation in Parliament. English warships had shut down ports and harbors, creating hardships and effectively strangling commerce. Virginians, Rhode Islanders, Bostonians, and New Yorkers began to feel more connected with the cities and states they had helped build than the distant land of their ancestors.

It is important to remember that, in spite of growing anger, no more than 35 percent of colonists actively participated in the rebellion at any one time. Many colonists still felt deeply connected with England. Twenty percent remained Loyalists throughout the war, and a plurality were undecided. The Patriots slowly attracted more of these fence-sitters as their cause gained momentum. Still, the Revolutionary War set neighbor against neighbor and divided families even more than the Civil War. Benjamin Franklin's own son was a Loyalist. Both sides were guilty of abuses and war crimes, but the opportunity to create an entirely new nation arose out of this deadly chaos.

The signing of the Declaration of Independence remains a landmark moment in human history, declaring for all to see that legitimate government derives its power from the consent of the governed. "We hold these truths to be self-evident, that all men are created equal, that they are endowed by their Creator with certain unalienable Rights, that among these are Life, Liberty and the pursuit of Happiness" set a precedent for all free governments to follow and remains an ideal toward which nations strive. All that being said, the Declaration is not, and never was, a governing document. It expressed unique ideals and opened the door to a bloody eight years of war that would test the Patriots' commitment to these principles. Next came years of argument, debate, and compromise as the 13 colonies formed an entirely new and unprecedented nation.

Rabbit Trails //

Answering the Cry for Freedom: Stories of African Americans and the American Revolution
by Gretchen Woelfle, illustrated by R. Gregory Christie
Even as American Patriots fought for independence from British rule during the Revolutionary War, oppressive conditions remained for the thousands of enslaved and free African Americans living in this country. But African Americans took up their own fight for freedom by joining the British and American armies, preaching, speaking out, and writing about the evils of slavery, and establishing settlements in Nova Scotia and Africa.

Benjamin Banneker: Brilliant Surveyor, Mathematician, and Astronomer by Erika Wittekind
A brief but detailed biography of the great self-taught mathematician and astronomer will help students learn more about this remarkable man and his mission to fight for equality.

Come All You Brave Soldiers: Blacks in the Revolutionary War
by Clinton Cox
In the Revolutionary War of the United States, black soldiers fought bravely for the freedom of a country that enslaved and oppressed them. Their story of courage and sacrifice is finally told.

The Great Little Madison by Jean Fritz
This life story of the father of the Constitution is a must for those doing constitutional studies. James Madison used his quiet eloquence, intelligence, and passion for colonial unification to help shape the Constitution.

Johnny Tremain: A Story of Boston in Revolt by Esther Forbes
This classic Newbery Medal winner takes readers into the heart of Boston during the Revolutionary War. In this engaging, fast-paced, and well-researched book, readers will meet Johnny, a young apprentice silversmith who jumps at the chance to participate with John Hancock and John and Samuel Adams in the exciting events that led to the Boston Tea Party and the Battle of Lexington.

Never Caught, the Story of Ona Judge, Young Readers Edition
by Erica Armstrong Dunbar and Kathleen Van Cleve
Born into a life of slavery, Ona Judge grew up in the shadows, both at the Washingtons' residence and in the first few decades of our new country. But times were changing. Although George Washington held incredibly conflicted views on the institution of slavery, more and more citizens and political figures were becoming vocal opponents of slavery. Follow Ona's journey as she escaped to freedom and fought the Washingtons' continued efforts to capture her. **Parental Warning:** There is one subtle reference to rape on page 11.

Character Connection //

SELF-GOVERNMENT: Martin Luther wrote in *On Christian Freedom*, "A Christian man is the most free lord of all, and subject to none; a Christian man is the most dutiful servant of all, and subject to every one." This seeming paradox is at the heart of the idea of Christian self-government. A free society established on the rule of law, such as we enjoy in the United States, requires self-government. For Christians, spiritual freedom, like that described by Luther, allows us to serve others, contribute to the common good, and exercise self-government to love our neighbors. It can even mean giving up our "rights" for the good of others.

Self-government, or self-control, begins at home, but the consequences are widespread. Consider the child who faithfully does his chores and completes his schoolwork without being told to do so. He experiences freedom from being told what to do, nagging, and punishment. If his parents are aware of and recognize his self-government, they will probably grant him additional rights and privileges within the home. The child who fights against every chore, argues with every suggestion, and bullies his way out of obligations will generally find that his rights and privileges become more and more limited. This happens on the city, state, and national levels as well. Outside of the inevitable injustices of living in a fallen world, a self-governed and generous population will enjoy more peace, freedom, and safety than a society made up of selfish, indulgent, and contentious individuals.

Read through the following verses as you move through this section and discuss them in light of examples of self-government and self-control that you encounter in the literature.

Proverbs 25:28
2 Timothy 1:7
2 Peter 1:5-7
James 1:19
Titus 2:11-12

The Age of Phillis by Honorée Fanonne Jeffers
Phillis Wheatley Peters was born free in West Africa but then captured, enslaved, and brought to Massachusetts as a young child. Yet, by the end of her life, she is again a free woman and the first female African American poet to have her works published. Readers will be drawn into this story as Jeffers uses her own poetry, excerpts of Wheatley's works, and quotes from primary sources to explore Phillis's life, private feelings, hopes, and dreams.

The Poems of Phillis Wheatley: With Letters and a Memoir by Phillis Wheatley
This reprint of Wheatley's memoir and poetry marks a pivotal moment in American literature. This is essential reading for any student of American literature.

What Are You Figuring Now?: A Story about Benjamin Banneker by Jeri Ferris
In 1791, plans for the new capital city, Washington, D.C., were in the works, but who would survey the new and unique city? Thomas Jefferson recommended Benjamin Banneker for the job. Banneker was a free black man who lived when black Americans had few, if any, rights. Yet he was an accomplished farmer, mathematician, astronomer, and surveyor.

The American Soldiers by H. Charles McBarron, Jr

Online Resources //

BENJAMIN FRANKLIN DOCUMENTARY

Access at "Benjamin Franklin: Author of the Declaration of Independence | Full Documentary | Biography" on the Biography YouTube channel.

JOHN ADAMS MINISERIES

Featuring Paul Giamatti and Laura Linney as John and Abigail Adams, *John Adams* is an excellent miniseries based on David McCullough's biography of the founding father. Students who watch this series will come to understand the incredible sacrifices made by the Adams family as well as gain an appreciation for the broken humanity of the brilliant Adams. **Parental Warning:** As always, preview for appropriateness. Available online or on DVD from many libraries.

MOUNT VERNON

This excellent website is a wealth of information on our first president, U.S. history, and more. www.mountvernon.org/

REVOLUTIONARY FOOD

Ever wonder what people ate during the Revolutionary War? Check out "What Foods Did Americans Eat During The Revolutionary War?" on the Weird History YouTube channel.

SLAVERY & THE PRESIDENTS

The following website, maintained by the White House Historical Association, offers a detailed interactive timeline showing the relationship between U.S. presidents and slavery. Read about the people enslaved in the households of eight U.S. presidents, as well as interesting tidbits like how hard it was for Abigail Adams to find a sober cook! www.whitehousehistory.org/spn/timeline

Activities & Handicraft //

WAX SEAL:

Sealing letters and important documents with wax helped keep things private for centuries! Make your own here: https://mypoppet.com.au/makes/diy-wax-seal-household-items/

PUNCHED TIN LANTERN:

Tin lanterns were essential for life in the Revolutionary War period.
Use the following instructions to make one: www.amrevmuseum.org/shine-your-light-with-our-punched-tin-craft

BULLET JOURNALING WITH GEORGE WASHINGTON:

George Washington kept meticulous journals throughout his life. Use the following activity from Mount Vernon to learn about bullet journaling and Washington's method of record-keeping:
www.mountvernon.org/education/lesson-plans/lesson/bullet-journaling-with-washington-2/

Creative Writing Prompt //

Create a discussion between two friends who find themselves on opposite sides during the Revolutionary War. This can be in the form of a play or conversation. Keep it civil and friendly!

Research Essays & Projects //

FEDERAL GOVERNMENT

The tension between the states and the federal government has plagued the nation from its very first days. There are benefits to this tension (the states help limit the power and reach of the federal government) as well as drawbacks. Research a current event that has set a state or group of states in opposition to the federal government. How would you resolve this issue?

FREEDOM

What does freedom mean to you? Choose a historical figure from your readings in this section and research their views on freedom and civic responsibility. As you research, consider your own understanding of freedom. Write an essay comparing and contrasting your view with that of the historical figure you chose. Record essay in the portfolio.

Join, or Die by Benjamin Franklin

BREAK UP WITH BRITAIN

Write a "Dear John" or breakup letter from the American colonies to England explaining why you think this relationship is no longer working. Use the historical facts you have been learning but make it funny!

LESSON 37

1. Introduce *Black Heroes of the American Revolution* by Burke Davis. Read pages vii-12. These pages introduce some of the enslaved and free Black men who took up arms in the Americans' fight for freedom. We will be learning more about these heroes as we move through this section. Discussion prompt:

> Many of the soldiers you read about never received payment or recognition for their service to the Revolutionary cause. Why do you think this was the case?

2. Read pages 181-194 of *George Washington's World*.

3. Which side would you have chosen during the Revolutionary War? The passage of time has diminished how fraught this situation was for most colonists. Explore the following links to understand a bit more about the weight of this decision and then discuss the benefits and drawbacks of each position.

> www.ncpedia.org/anchor/which-side-take
> "Would You Have Joined the American Revolution?" on the Origin of Everything YouTube channel

> If you would like to dig deeper, gather some friends and family members and set up a friendly debate with talking points provided in this handout from the National Parks Service:
> www.nps.gov/mocr/learn/education/upload/Lesson-1.pdf

LESSON 38

1. Read pages 110-123 of *Poor Richard*. Discussion prompt:

> Benjamin Franklin lived many of the ideals that came to be central to American identity: freedom-loving, hard-working, community-minded, and curious. Discuss how that American identity has remained the same and how it has changed. What do you think Benjamin Franklin would think of American politics today?

2. Read pages 198-204 of *George Washington's World*.

3. Choose a project from the Activities & Handicraft section, to the left, and begin working on it.

LESSON 39

1. Finish reading *Poor Richard*. This reading takes us forward in time, but we will be circling back to finish our study of the Revolutionary War.

2. To this point, we have read about battles, political maneuvering, and other aspects of the American Revolution. Our next book will help us understand what it was like to live during the war, right at the epicenter of British power in the colonies: New York City. Introduce *Sophia's War: A Tale of the Revolution* by Avi. Begin by reading the note on page 1 and Chapters 1-5. Discussion and narration prompts:

> To learn more about Nathan Hale, watch "Nathan Hale: Who's Who in the American Revolution I AF-178" on the Ancestral Findings YouTube channel

> Sophia refers to Thomas Paine as a "radical." Discuss her use of this term. Do you agree? Does your context influence your opinion? How would you describe a "radical" today?

3. Create a new section in the portfolio titled "Sophia's War." Copy the maps at the beginning of *Sophia's War* and paste them into the portfolio.

Black Revolutionaries

Caesar Tarrant

James Forten

Agrippa Hull

Lemuel Haynes

Peter Salem

LESSON 40

1. Read Chapters 6-10 of *Sophia's War*. Discussion prompt:

> Forced quartering of English soldiers was one of the colonists' many complaints against England. What did this practice reveal about the English government's opinion of its colonists' rights to private property, freedom of movement, and privacy? What do you think it would feel like to have unwanted guests forced upon you, whether you supported their mission or not?

2. Read Chapter 2 of *Black Heroes of the American Revolution*. **Parental Warning:** This chapter references a historical quote with a racial slur on page 18.

3. Read pages 205-214 of *George Washington's World*.

LESSON 41

1. Read Chapters 11-16 of *Sophia's War*. Discussion and narration prompts:

> Describe John André. What do you think of him? Contrast him with Sophia's brother, William.

> On page 68, André states that Sophia should put her mind to "making yourself as agreeable to me as possible." How does this demand strike you? Does it also reflect what the British monarchy and Parliament thought was the proper role of the colonies to their imperial master? How does this attitude violate Sophia's dignity and worth?

> Times of war have consistently expanded opportunities for women. Discuss why this is and what changes it led to for Sophia. How is this new world imagined by Thomas Paine as "a blank sheet" that provides Sophia ways to be something more than "agreeable"?

2. Mark the following on the map in the portfolio:

New York City   Hudson River   West Point, NY

3. Finish writing your research paper and add it to the portfolio.

4. Read pages 215-224 of *George Washington's World*.

LESSON 42

1. Read Chapter 3 of *Black Heroes of the American Revolution*.

2. The British prison ships were horrific. Over 11,000 Patriots died aboard these vessels during the Revolutionary War, more than the total land battle fatalities. Learn more about the *Jersey*, where James Forten was held for months, as well as other prison ships and the brave men and boys who were kept aboard them. There is also an incredible story of a woman who tried to help prisoners escape!

- "Prisoners Of War I American Revolution" on the Quest T.V. YouTube channel
- www.history.com/news/british-prison-ships-american-revolution-hms-jersey
- https://nylandmarks.org/explore-ny/the-prison-ship-martyrs-monument/

3. The trial of the British soldiers following the Boston Massacre is a fascinating legal moment in American history. Check out www.masshist.org/features/massacre/trials.

4. Read Chapters 17-22 of *Sophia's War*.

LESSON 43

1. Read Chapters 23-28 of *Sophia's War*. Narration and discussion prompts:

Describe the conditions Sophia witnessed in the prisons and aboard the *Good Intent*.

The British treatment of prisoners of war during the Revolution was horrific. In their minds, these rebels were not revolutionaries fighting for the cause of freedom; they were simply traitors to their nation. Discuss how this mindset and perspective allowed them to dehumanize the Americans.

Summarize the main aspects of Part One of *Sophia's War*.

2. Choose a project from the Activities & Handicraft section on page 56 and begin working on it.

3. Check out the following article to learn more about the Sugar House in New York City:
https://untappedcities.com/2013/07/25/daily-what-revolutionary-war-sugar-house-prison-window-downtown-manhattan/

LESSON 44

1. Begin Part Two of *Sophia's War* and read Chapters 29-39. Narration and discussion prompts:

Sophia's interactions with Mr. Townsend caused her to recall the following proverb: "Wise heads have quiet tongues and eager ears." Discuss this adage. Do you think it is true?

In the 18th century, girls had minimal opportunities. Sophia already experienced a surprise benefit of wartime in working as a printer's assistant to help support her family. Since girls and women were generally thought of in strictly domestic terms, Sophia has an advantage as a spy because she is usually unnoticed and easily overlooked as a teenage girl. What other members of society at this time would have made good spies?

2. Read Chapter 5 of *Black Heroes of the American Revolution*. We will return to Chapter 4 later.

LESSON 45

1. Read Chapters 40-50 of *Sophia's War*. Discussion and narration prompts:

Describe how the elite British commanders lived in New York during the war and contrast this with the living conditions of most New Yorkers at the time.

Why was it so hard for Sophia to comprehend Benedict Arnold's treason? Consider the way she described him throughout the story up to this point.

Sophia wrote, "Hearing truth makes many deaf." Discuss this idea. Can you think of examples of this in the world today?

2. Mr. Townsend was part of the Culper Spy Ring, an intelligence-gathering group that reported to General Washington. Learn more about them by watching "Long Island History - Ep. 2, Culper Spy Ring" on the Eric Simonson YouTube channel.

1. *Baron Steuben Drilling Troops at Valley Forge* by Edwin Austin Abbey, c. 1911
2. *Bunker Hill* by Howard Pyle

 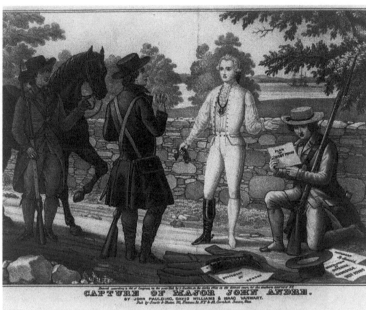

CAPTURE OF MAJOR JOHN ANDRE.

ONE OF THE TREASON LETTERS IN CYPHER

1. *John André* 2. *Capture of Major John André* by John Paulding, David Williams & Isaac Van Wart
3. Cipher letter by Benedict Arnold 4. *Benedict Arnold* by Thomas Hart, 1776

LESSON 46

1. Read Chapters 51-60 of *Sophia's War*.

2. Using the map at the beginning of *Sophia's War*, mark the following on your map of North America:

Teller's Point	Peekskill	Fort Lafayette
Tarrytown	White Plains	Dobb's Ferry
Tappan	King's Ferry	Verplanck's Point

3. Sophia worked for General Howe at Beekman Mansion. The history of this home is fascinating. Learn more here: http://daytoninmanhattan.blogspot.com/2011/09/lost-1763-beekman-mansion-mount.html

4. Read pages 228-231, up to "Cornwallis Surrenders," of *George Washington's World*.

LESSON 47

1. Finish reading *Sophia's War*. Discussion and narration prompts:

Compare André's treatment as a prisoner of war with how William was treated at the Sugar House.

Most Revolutionary War information centers on Boston and other Patriot strongholds. What did you learn about the New York City front by reading *Sophia's War*?

Describe Sophia's transformation from idealistic Patriot girl to a woman who knows the cost of her convictions and principles.

2. Return to the very beginning of *Sophia's War* and re-read the reader's note on page 1. Sophia asks you to decide if she made the right decisions. Write a brief answer to her question, "Was I right to act in such a way?" Record your answer in the portfolio.

3. The treachery of Benedict Arnold has perplexed many for a long time. Research his shift from Patriot hero to reviled traitor and record your findings in the portfolio. The following video will be helpful: "Benedict Arnold: The Revolutionary War in Four Minutes" on the American Battlefield Trust YouTube channel.

4. Read the following article to learn more about André:
https://allthingsliberty.com/2018/08/the-death-and-resurrection-of-major-john-andre/

LESSON 48

1. Thwarting Benedict Arnold's treason was key to the ultimate Patriot victory. Read pages 231-235 of *George Washington's World*. The Patriots won, and a new nation was born!

2. Read Chapter 4 of *Black Heroes of the American Revolution*. Discussion and narration prompts:

The Marquis de Lafayette found that the colonists in Virginia were unwilling to help his troops. Given Lafayette's passion for the American cause, discuss how he may have felt about the Virginians' reluctance to help his soldiers.

Learn more about the incredible James Armistead Lafayette by watching "A Conversation with James Armistead Lafayette" on the Colonial Williamsburg YouTube channel.

Discuss why Armistead joined the fight for American freedom at significant risk to himself and with no promise of personal benefit. Did he have a choice?

LESSON 48 continued

3. Research and write a report on James Armistead Lafayette's life and service to the United States. Add to the portfolio.

4. For a review of the battles of the Revolutionary War as well as an in-depth look at the battle at Yorktown, watch the following videos:

www.battlefields.org/learn/maps/revolutionary-war-animated-map

"Now Or Never: Yorktown Campaign of 1781 (Full Movie)" on George Washington's Mount Vernon YouTube channel.

LESSON 49

1. Read pages 236-244 of *George Washington's World*. The new nation had to form a government and solve a whole host of problems. In the next section, we will be studying the Constitutional Congress and the years of debate that led to our unique republican form of government.

2. Read Chapter 6 of *Black Heroes of the American Revolution*. Discussion and narration prompts:

Describe the obstacles faced by Black veterans following the Revolutionary War.

Discuss Harriet Beecher Stowe's quote on page 75.

3. Choose one figure from *Black Heroes of the American Revolution* to research. Write and record a brief biography in the portfolio.

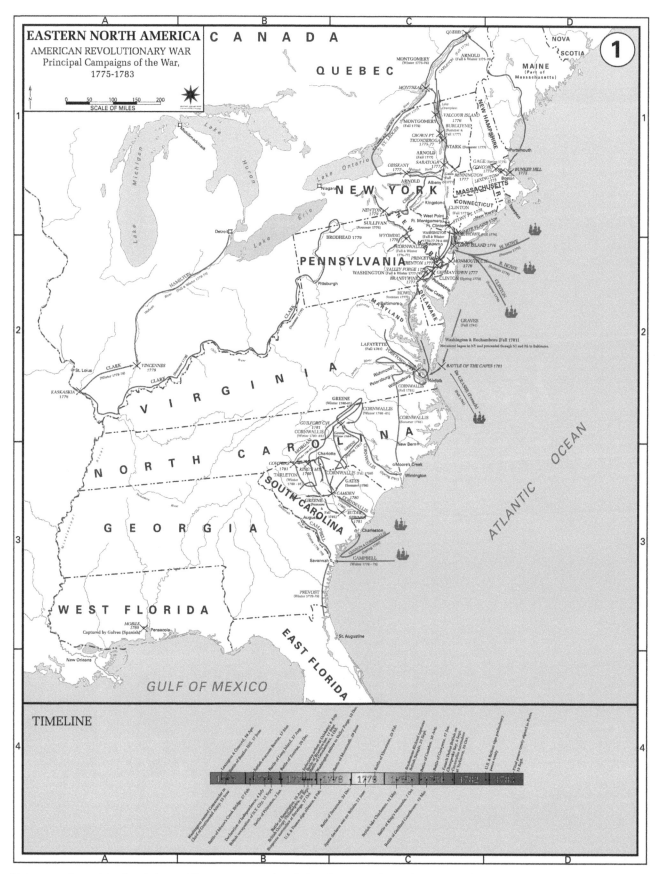

Major campaigns of the Revolutionary War: www.westpoint.edu/academics/academic-departments/history/american-revolution
Click on "Major Campaigns of the American Revolutionary War."

PART V

The
Young United States
1783–1864

The Rocky Mountains, Lander's Peak by Albert Bierstadt, 1863

$\mathcal{E}$merging from seven years of war, the new nation was weary but optimistic and ready to prove itself to the world. The first task at hand was making sure the world recognized the United States as a sovereign nation. Delegates hurried to Paris to draft treaties with England, France, Spain, and other European powers. They sought trade agreements and argued and debated for months. Eventually, treaties between the 13 states and the European nations were signed, and the delegates returned home, only to face the even more significant challenge of recreating the entire government. The Continental Congress returned to Philadelphia to address conflict between the states, seek ways to pay the nation's debts, and address weighty questions of power, states' rights, slavery, and more. We will learn about the unique government they created through debate, compromise, and dogged realism.

The new nation was buoyant, hopeful, and energetic. The opportunity to pursue happiness was guaranteed to all citizens (at that time, white, land-owning men). Many took on that challenge, investing in their own futures and thus strengthening their nation. And the young country needed this energy, as it immediately faced challenges: an epidemic, continued attacks on American ships by the English, debt, and other pressures. Would the United States rise to these challenges? The answer was a resounding "Yes!"

Industry flourished, and technological innovation gave rise to cities throughout the north. As the nation's third president, Thomas Jefferson oversaw the Louisiana Purchase, and the borders of the United States suddenly leaped to the west. Lewis and Clark's Corps of Discovery fired the imaginations of young families up and down the Eastern Seaboard, and thousands decided to pursue their fortunes in these uncharted territories, escaping the now crowded, and sometimes dire, conditions in the factories that were propelling the economy forward.

The discovery of gold in California spurred even more movement west. It attracted prospectors from all over the world, and California entered the country as the most diverse state, a powerhouse of innovation and positivity. The Pony Express briefly connected east and west for 18 mythic months before being replaced by the telegraph. And shortly after that, the Transcontinental Railroad was completed.

The thirst for land meant that hundreds of thousands of Indigenous people were driven off their ancestral lands and relocated to reservations, where their traditions and cultural practices were threatened and often lost. We will look at the Trail of Tears and how the western movement forever altered the lives of the diverse tribes who had called this country home long before European arrival.

In the South, the enslaved populations continued to support the nation by providing the raw materials required by the industrial boom while being denied their freedoms. For freedom-loving groups like the Quakers and abolitionists, the plight of these men, women, and children—nearly 20 percent of the country's population—drove their passion for seeing slavery abolished. This led to the expansion and development of the Underground Railroad and the rise of Black abolitionists like Sojourner Truth and Frederick Douglass. They carried on the work of Olaudah Equiano and Phillis Wheatley.

We will now turn our attention to Philadelphia during the hot days of the Constitutional Convention.

Rabbit Trails //

Amistad: The Slave Uprising Aboard the Spanish Schooner by Helen Kromer
Nearly 160 years ago, a group of kidnapped Africans aboard the Spanish slave ship *La Amistad* revolted and attempted to set sail for home. Instead, after being misguided by the ship's navigator to the coast of New England, the charismatic leader Cinque and his companions found themselves embroiled in an international debate. *Amistad* is an unforgettable story for readers of all ages.

An American Plague: The True and Terrifying Story of the Yellow Fever Epidemic of 1793 by Jim Murphy
Philadelphia, 1793: The capital of the United States and the largest city in North America is devastated by an apparently incurable disease, cause unknown. Drawing on firsthand accounts, critically acclaimed author Jim Murphy spotlights the heroic role of Philadelphia's free Black citizens in combating yellow fever, the efforts and intrigues of doctors and politicians—among them George Washington—and the search for the fever's causes and cure, not found for more than a century afterward. Thoroughly researched, unflinching in its discussion of medical details, and generously illustrated with archival prints and photographs, this award-winning account offers a glimpse into life in the United States in the years immediately following our nation's birth while drawing timely parallels to modern-day epidemics.

Facing Frederick: The Life of Frederick Douglass, a Monumental American Man by Tonya Bolden
Drawing on new scholarship, 19th-century newspapers, a collection of Douglass's correspondence, and other resources, Bolden's biography captures what a multifaceted man Douglass was, his incredible talent, and his fascinating life.

Freedom Roads: Searching for the Underground Railroad
by Joyce Hansen and Gary McGowan, illustrated by James Ransome
The Underground Railroad was meant to be a set of secret pathways, and its traces have been obscured by time. In this book, the authors show how archaeologists and historians sift through corn cobs and root cellars, study songs and quilts, and use the latest technology to reconstruct those heroic journeys. *Freedom Roads* offers a fresh look at the escape routes from slavery and introduces the tools, methods, and insights of archaeology, anthropology, and historical conservation. Here is a modern-day detective story that uncovers the traces of a time in American history when courageous slaves and idealistic abolitionists defied the law and saved lives.

Harriet Tubman: Conductor on the Underground Railroad by Ann Petry
Harriet Tubman was born in slavery and dreamed of being free. She was willing to risk everything—including her own life—to see that dream come true. After her daring escape, Harriet became a conductor on the secret Underground Railroad, helping others make the dangerous journey to freedom. This award-winning introduction to the abolitionist, which was named an ALA Notable Book and an Outstanding Book, includes additional educational back matter such as a timeline, discussion questions, and extension activities.

Harriet Tubman, Secret Agent: How Daring Slaves and Free Blacks Spied for the Union During the Civil War
by Thomas Allen
This compelling biography tells the amazing tale of Harriet Tubman using details uncovered from military and intelligence archives, diaries, and little-known memoirs from ex-slaves. In a compelling narrative, surprising new facts about Harriet's story are brought to light: readers discover that the ex-slave who led hundreds to freedom along the Underground Railroad was also a spy for the Union Army.

Heart of a Samurai by Margi Preus
In 1841, a Japanese fishing vessel sank, and its crew had to swim to a small, unknown island, where they were rescued by a passing American ship. Japan's borders were closed to all Western nations, so the crew sets off to America, learning English on the way. Manjiro, a 14-year-old boy, is curious and eager to learn everything he can about this new culture. Eventually, the captain adopts Manjiro and takes him to his home in New England. The boy lives there for some time and then heads to San Francisco to pan for gold. This is a true story you should not miss.

Indian Heroes and Great Chieftains by Charles A. Eastman OhiyeS'a
This book presents biographies of 15 great Native American chiefs, including Crazy Horse, Sitting Bull, and Red Cloud. Most of the chiefs presented were Sioux, and some of them were Eastman's friends, such as Rain-In-The-Face.

In the Shadow of Liberty: The Hidden History of Slavery, Four Presidents, and Five Black Lives by Kenneth C. Davis
Did you know that many of America's Founding Fathers—who fought for liberty and justice for all—were slave owners? Through the powerful stories of five enslaved people who were "owned" by four of our greatest presidents, this middle-grade nonfiction book helps set the record straight about the role slavery played in the founding of America.

Narrative of the Life of Frederick Douglass, an American Slave by Frederick Douglass
Incidents in the Life of a Slave Girl by Harriet Jacobs
These are two of the most influential African American slave narratives, crucial works that illuminate and inform the other. These books reveal the brutalities of slavery in stark detail, as well as the strength of the human spirit in overcoming devastating hardship.

Nothing Like It in the World by Stephen E. Ambrose
The U.S. government pitted two companies—the Union Pacific and the Central Pacific Railroads—against each other in a race for funding, encouraging speed over caution. At its peak, the workforce approached the size of Civil War armies, with as many as 15,000 workers on each line. The surveyors, the men who picked the route, lived off buffalo, deer, and antelope. Nothing like this great work had ever been seen in the world when the last spike, a golden one, was driven in at Promontory Peak, Utah, in 1869, as the Central Pacific and the Union Pacific tracks were joined.

Indians Discovering Lewis and Clark by Charles Marion Russell

Riders of the Pony Express by Ralph Moody
Prior to the Civil War, the fastest mail between the West Coast and the East took almost 30 days by stagecoach along a southern route through Texas. Some Californians feared their state would not remain in the Union, separated so far from the free states. Informed by his intimate knowledge of horses and Western geography, Ralph Moody's exciting account of the 18 critical months that the Pony Express service operated between April 1860 and October 1861 pays tribute to the true grit and determination of the riders and horses of the Pony Express.

Sacajawea by Joseph Bruchac
At just 16 years old, Sacajawea had already been kidnapped, had been gambled away to a French trader who wanted her for his wife, and was pregnant with her first child. But her greatest challenge was about to begin. As Captains Meriwether Lewis and William Clark started their journey to forge a path from the Mississippi River to the Pacific Ocean, Sacajawea served as their guide, translator, and peacemaker. Join these intrepid explorers as they establish trade with Native Americans; navigate uncharted territory; battle wild animals, warrior tribes, and disease; and live to tell the tale. Told from the varied perspectives of Sacajawea, Lewis, and Clark, this should not be missed!

Sequoyah: The Cherokee Man Who Gave His People Writing by James Rumford
Although this is a picture book, it tells the amazing story of an ordinary man with an extraordinary idea—to create a writing system for the Cherokee Indians and turn his people into a nation of readers and writers. The task he set for himself was daunting. Sequoyah knew no English and had no idea how to capture speech on paper. But slowly and painstakingly, ignoring the hoots and jibes of his neighbors and friends, he worked out a system that surprised the Cherokee Nation—and the world of the 1820s—with its beauty and simplicity.

The True Confessions of Charlotte Doyle by Avi
Life aboard a trading ship in the early 19th century was hard, sometimes violent, and not the place you would expect to find an educated young lady. This story paints an exciting picture of life aboard a ship and weaves a tale that may not be entirely historically accurate, but it is a lot of fun to read.

Why We Serve: Native Americans in the United States Armed Forces
This book commemorates the 2020 opening of the National Native American Veterans Memorial at the Smithsonian National Museum of the American Indian, the first landmark in Washington, D.C., to recognize the bravery and sacrifice of Native veterans. American Indians' history of military service dates to colonial times, and today, they serve at one of the highest rates of any ethnic group. *Why We Serve* explores the range of reasons why, from love of their home to an expression of their warrior traditions. The book brings fascinating history to life with historical photographs, sketches, paintings, and maps. Incredible contributions from important voices in the field offer a complex examination of the history of Native American service.

Activities & Handicraft //

BUILD A CORPS OF DISCOVERY DIORAMA

If you would like to build a Lewis and Clark Expedition diorama, Imex makes one titled "Lewis & Clark Expedition Set IMXS0523." It is available on Amazon or at Hobby Lobby. These are tiny miniatures that are historically accurate and include the key Corp members, Sacajawea, canoes, tepees, horses, and so forth. If you have a student who loves to work with tiny miniature worlds, this would be an enjoyable project to do together.

STAGE A PLAY

The play *George Washington's Spectacles* explores the tense days following the British surrender at Yorktown as the soldiers, some of whom had fought for six years, looked to Congress to pay them for their long service. Can General Washington keep his frustrated men from outright rebellion? Download the script and instructions here: https://classroommagazines.scholastic.com/content/dam/classroom-magazines/magazines/promotion/JS-1-021317-GeneralWashingtonsSpectacles.pdf

DIAGNOSING AND TREATING YELLOW FEVER IN PHILADELPHIA

The Historical Society of Pennsylvania has put together a detailed unit study focusing on the various methods used by doctors during the yellow fever epidemic of 1793. Using original and primary source documents, students can study symptoms, determine treatment plans, and evaluate the effectiveness of Dr. Rush's bloodletting therapies.

www.portal.hsp.org/unit-plan-items/unit-plan-24

EXPLORE ABOLITIONISM TODAY

Slavery still flourishes today with over 40,000,000 people enslaved around the world. Learn more about how you can help at the following websites:

www.ijm.org

www.a21.org

Write a letter to your elected representative explaining your position on this issue and what action you would like them to pursue to end modern-day slavery.

SALT DOUGH-IT!

Creating a salt dough map of your state or the entire United States is a fun project and allows you to explore topography and geography. Search for salt dough recipes online and use an outline map to help you get the right shape. Once you've formed the map and let it dry, paint it to reflect geographical features.

Character Connection //

COURAGE: This section features many stories of courageous action and brave determination. Sometimes courage means staying in a disease-ridden city when you could flee to safety. Or it's leading enslaved people to freedom at significant personal risk. It can be standing against state-sponsored injustice or listening to someone tell their heartbreaking story. Courage takes many forms, and we will read about selfless people who loved and served bravely. As you read through these accounts, consider the following Bible verses:

Deuteronomy 31:6

Joshua 1:6-9

1 Chronicles 28:20

Psalm 27:14

Psalm 31:24

Psalm 46:1

Isaiah 41:10

Philippians 4:13

1 Corinthians 16:13

2 Timothy 1:7

Creative Writing Prompt //

Imagine you are one of the delegates sent to the Constitutional Convention in 1787, and write three letters home from Philadelphia describing what took place there over that long, hot summer. Describe the weather, what it felt like to sit hour after hour in the closed hot Assembly Room, which delegates you agreed with and which ones annoyed you. Have fun with these letters.

Research Essays & Projects //

PANDEMIC, NOW AND THEN: Pandemics and plagues generally follow a similar pattern as they spread throughout communities. Compare the yellow fever epidemic of 1793 with the Covid-19 pandemic of 2020-2022. What rumors circulated in Philadelphia? What misinformation spread via the internet during Covid? How were peoples' reactions similar or different? Looking back to 1793, were there lessons from 1793 Philadelphia that could have guided a better response to Covid-19 in 2020? Record your thoughts and findings in the portfolio.

FREE AFRICAN SOCIETY OF PHILADELPHIA: Research the founding of this critical and historic society and its impact on American culture at large. Include details on the lives of its founders, Richard Allen and Absalom Jones.

ALONG THE TRAIL WITH LEWIS AND CLARK: Write a first-person narrative about the Corps of Discovery from the perspective of either an expedition member, Sacajawea, or a Native tribe member who encounters the group. The following article may be helpful: www.hcn.org/issues/280/14923

Online Resources //

JAMES MADISON, CONSTITUTIONALIST
Madison's contribution to the Constitution cannot be overstated.
Explore the following website to learn more about this intellectual giant:

https://learningenglish.voanews.com/a/james-madison-father-of-constitution/2883722.html

LEWIS & CLARK NATIONAL PARK SERVICE SITES
Check out sites along the Lewis and Clark trail and learn more about the expedition.

www.nps.gov/subjects/travellewisandclark/visit.htm

GOVERNMENT STRUCTURE
We will be going over basic governmental structure and legislative process in this section.
If you would like to dig deeper, check out these two sources:

Khan Academy provides a detailed course at
www.khanacademy.org/humanities/us-government-and-civics/

Sharon Says So offers fun workshops for immediate download at:
https://education.sharonmcmahon.com/collections/recording

UNDERGROUND RAILROAD
The following resources provide information on the Underground Railroad and the heroic people who traveled its paths:

www.eiu.edu/eiutps/underground_railroad.php
https://www.historynet.com/underground-railroad
https://www.nationalgeographic.org/encyclopedia/underground-railroad/

WAR OF 1812
Explore the background, battles, and key figures in the fraught War of 1812:

https://amhistory.si.edu/starspangledbanner/the-war-of-1812.aspx
www.loc.gov/rr/program/bib/1812/

1. *Washington as Statesman at the Constitutional Convention* by Junius Brutus Stearns
2. Assembly room at Independence Hall, Philadelphia

LESSON 50

1. The Revolutionary War was finally over, and the United States had emerged as an independent nation. Exhausted from the war, General Washington happily headed home to Mount Vernon to rest. Read pages 245-255 and 261-263 of *George Washington's World*. Discussion prompts:

These pages create an idyllic picture of life at Mount Vernon and Monticello. The lifeblood of these plantations was the enslaved labor of Black people. Both Washington and Jefferson, brilliant leaders that they were, supported slavery and benefited from it. While we would love to think that they were kind enslavers (that idea itself is a misnomer), the historical record proves otherwise. It is important to remember that actual historical facts are not character assassination. Historical inquiry and curiosity allow us to see men and women for who they indeed are. Jefferson was a brilliant polymath whose words articulated ideas that had long lain in the hearts of mankind. Washington was a noble president, the faithful and beloved father of our nation. These are both accurate and indisputable facts. And yet, Jefferson and Washington enslaved people, and the record shows that they were not kind slavers. Knowing both facts gives us a fuller representation of these two men and human nature. It reminds us not to idolize people, and it helps us maintain a view of the past untinged with nostalgia. To learn more about Washington's treatment of the enslaved people who worked for him, check out *Never Caught, The Story of Ona Judge, Young Readers Edition* (see Rabbit Trails on page 54 for full description). To learn more about Thomas Jefferson and slavery, read the following article:
www.monticello.org/slavery/slavery-faqs/property/

Discuss the conflict between the ideals of freedom and equality held dear by Washington and Jefferson and their roles as enslavers.

2. When the colonies declared their independence, they operated as a group of individual and distinct states united to wage war for independence. This was accomplished with the Articles of Confederation. Learn more about this critical first "constitution" of the United States here:
www.khanacademy.org/humanities/ap-us-history/period-3/articles-of-confederation-ush-lesson/v/the-articles-of-confederation

3. Negotiating the Treaty of Paris in 1783 was uniquely challenging and exposed the weaknesses of the Articles of Confederation. Learn more by watching "The 1783 Treaty of Paris in a Nutshell" on the Dave Benner YouTube channel.

LESSON 51

1. Read pages 267-269 and 279-288 of *George Washington's World*.

2. Shays' Rebellion was a turning point in U.S. history. It forced the individual states to recognize that their fear of a strong centralized federal government was hurting and weakening the nation. Learn more by watching "The Articles of Confederation and Shays' Rebellion" on the Khan Academy YouTube channel. "The Making of the American Constitution - Judy Walton" on the TedEd YouTube channel is also helpful.

LESSON 52

1. We will now study the structure of our government. Cut out the infographics on pages 109 and 111 and add them to your portfolio. These will serve as visual aids to understanding various aspects of our unique republic. We will be utilizing videos from several useful sources to help explain the information on these charts. A helpful reference for government structure can be found here: www.usa.gov/branches-of-government.

2. Create a new section in the portfolio titled "The Second Constitutional Convention and the Governance of the United States."

3. Watch "Social Contract" at www.khanacademy.org/humanities/us-government-and-civics/us-gov-foundations. Narration and discussion prompt:

Describe the "social contract." Why is it necessary for the existence of government?

Based on the social contract, you must give up some rights, along with the other citizens, to empower the government to protect rights that are very important to you. Which rights or freedoms are you most concerned with protecting? Which rights would you be willing to give up to protect those rights?

4. Watch "The United States Constitution and Bill of Rights" on the Ryan Hill YouTube channel and "The Constitutional Convention" on the Khan Academy YouTube channel. Study the Three Branches infographic and the Checks and Balances infographic on pages 109 and 111 of this guide.

LESSON 53

1. Compromise is central to good governance. In a nation of diverse opinions and convictions, debate, critical thinking, and compromise are fundamentally essential to the survival of a nation. When we look back at the Second Continental Congress, two compromises stand out: the Three-Fifths Compromise and the decision to put off resolving the issue of slavery. The following videos provide a good explanation of how these compromises were reached and their far-reaching consequences:

"Constitutional compromises: The Three-Fifths Compromise | U.S. government and civics | Khan Academy" on the Khan Academy YouTube channel.
"The U.S. Constitution, 3/5, and the Slave Trade Clause: Crash Course Black American History #9" on the CrashCourse YouTube channel.

Once you have watched both videos, discuss the reasons behind the decisions made by the delegates regarding the importation of enslaved people and counting the enslaved population. Dr. Clint Smith points out that nearly half the delegates owned enslaved people, and yet, the nation they were able to create would go on to provide unprecedented opportunities to millions of people. The fact that this future was built in part on the lives and sacrifices of enslaved Blacks is a part of our history and being able to hold these two truths is part of being a historian. Do you think these compromises were necessary? Articulate your position using historical evidence.

LESSON 54

1. We will now learn about the creation of laws or the legislative process. Check out the following sites:
www.usa.gov/how-laws-are-made
"How a bill becomes a law I U.S. government and civics I U.S. government and civics I Khan Academy"
"Diagramming how a bill becomes a law in the U.S." on the Khan Academy YouTube channel

2. Using the infographic on page 113 as a reference, draw your own illustration showing how a bill becomes a law. Add to your portfolio.

3. Look over pages 290-291 of *George Washington's World* and read pages 303-313. Discussion and narration prompts:

Discuss Hamilton's desire to ensure that the U.S. paid its debts. Why was this so important to him?

A new nation has no traditions or established ceremonies, and this lack of protocol resulted in some awkward situations for the first presidents. Discuss how tradition, social rules, and standards of etiquette help eliminate social missteps.

Discuss Thomas Paine's quote from page 310: "When it can be said in any country in the world: My poor are happy; neither ignorance nor distress is to be found among them; my jails are empty of prisoners, my streets of beggars; the aged are not in want, the taxes are not oppressive; when these things can be said, then may that country boast of its constitution and its government."

For anyone interested in learning more about the history of U.S. government debt, the following article is helpful:
www.theatlantic.com/business/archive/2012/11/the-long-story-of-us-debt-from-1790-to-2011-in-1-little-chart/265185/

LESSON 55

1. Read pages 314-315, 322-326 of *George Washington's World*.

> Discuss President Washington's decision to maintain neutrality. Do you agree with Washington's decision? If not, why? What would you have done in his position?

2. Benjamin Banneker's challenge to Thomas Jefferson marks the second time a Black person challenged Jefferson's false notions of African racial inferiority. Jefferson first minimized the accomplishments of Phillis Wheatley but took the time to respond to Banneker. Learn more about their exchange and read the entire text of their letters here:

> www.facinghistory.org/nobigotry/readings/created-equal

3. 1793 was a very busy year for the nation. In February, just before Congress recessed for a break, it passed the Fugitive Slave Act. George Washington began his second term in office on March 4. On April 22, he declared the United States neutral in the face of expanding European wars. Learn more about these important events at the following resources:

> www.mountvernon.org/library/digitalhistory/digital-encyclopedia/article/neutrality-proclamation/

> "The Fugitive Slave Act of 1793: Crash Course Black American History #10" on the CrashCourse YouTube channel

4. The energetic atmosphere in Philadelphia would give way to panic soon. Introduce *Fever 1793* by Laurie Halse Anderson. Read Chapters 1-5. Discussion and narration prompts:

> Describe Philadelphia at this time.

> Describe Matilda's relationship with her mother. What adjectives would you use to help someone understand Matilda's character?

> Relate the conversations between Grandfather and his friends in the coffee-house. How did the men react to the news of rising death counts?

5. Create a new section in the portfolio titled "Yellow Fever, Philadelphia, 1793."

LESSON 56

1. In *Fever 1793* Matilda recollects seeing "Blanchard's balloon." Research the historic first flight and record your findings in the portfolio.

2. Read Chapters 6-10 of *Fever 1793*. Research and narration prompts:

> Matilda's friend, Nathaniel, was apprenticed to a very famous American artist, Charles Willson Peale. Peale painted some of the most famous portraits of George Washington, Thomas Jefferson, and other historically significant Americans. If desired, visit the following link to learn more: www.mountvernon.org/library/digitalhistory/digital-encyclopedia/article/charles-willson-peale/

> Eliza was a member of the Free African Society of Philadelphia. Research the history of this organization and record your findings in the portfolio.

> Discuss the advice given by the College of Physicians (page 58 of *Fever 1793*) and compare it to the advice given during the Covid-19 pandemic of 2020-2021. What similarities and differences stand out most to you?

States & Territories of the United States of America

March 4, 1789 - August 7, 1789

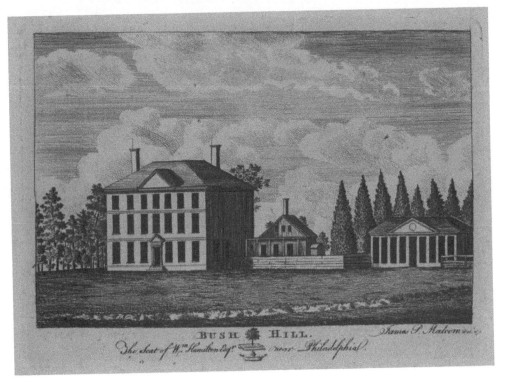

1. Elfreth's Alley, in Old City, Philadelphia, Pennsylvania
2. *Bush Hill* by James Peller Malcolm, c. 1792.

LESSON 57

1. Read Chapters 11-15 of *Fever 1793*. Discussion and narration prompts:

Describe the various ways that people reacted to the outbreak of yellow fever. Do crises like this have a way of revealing people's true character?

How has Matilda changed? Think back to Lesson 55 when you described Matilda's character. What words would you use now?

2. Watch the following tour of key sites in Philadelphia related to the Yellow Fever outbreak: "Fever: 1793 - A Virtual Tour with Sam Katz" on the Philadelphia: The Great Experiment YouTube channel.

3. Write out "Pestilence" by Philip Freneau and add it to the portfolio.

> "Pestilence"
> By Philip Freneau
>
> Hot, dry winds forever blowing,
> Dead men to the grave-yards going:
> Constant hearses,
> Funeral verses;
> Oh! what plagues—there is no knowing!
>
> Priests retreating from their pulpits!—
> Some in hot, and some in cold fits
> In bad temper,
> Off they scamper,
> Leaving us—unhappy culprits!
>
> Doctors raving and disputing,
> Death's pale army still recruiting—
> What a pother
> One with t'other!
> Some a-writing, some a-shooting.
>
> Nature's poisons here collected,
> Water, earth, and air infected—
> O, what pity,
> Such a City,
> Was in such a place erected!

Richard Allen

Matthew Clarkson

Absalom Jones

Benjamin Rush

LESSON 58

1. Read Chapters 16-19 of *Fever, 1793*.

At the end of the reading, Matilda found herself completely alone. Discuss the challenges this presents. What would you do in her situation?

2. As with all pandemics, doctors and civil leaders in Philadelphia disagreed vehemently on how to address the many issues and problems created by the yellow fever outbreak. Treatments were politicized and fiercely debated. Amid the devastation and societal breakdown, several figures stand out for their selfless service and courageous action. Choose one person from the following list to research. Over the next week, use your research to draft a biography on the person you chose.

Reverend Richard Allen
Mayor Matthew Clarkson
Dr. Jean Deveze
Stephen Girard
Peter Helm
Reverend Absalom Jones
Dr. Benjamin Rush
Mrs. Mary Saville

LESSON 59

1. Read Chapters 20-23 of *Fever 1793*.

2. Watch "Fever (1793-1820) - Philadelphia: The Great Experiment" and "Fever: 1793 - Richard Allen: Apostle of Freedom" on the Philadelphia: The Great Experiment YouTube channel.

3. Continue research on your biography project.

LESSON 60

1. Finish reading *Fever 1793*. Be sure to read through the Appendix. This is a more extended reading assignment, so take a couple of days to complete it. Discussion and narration prompts:

Narrate the differences between Dr. Rush's treatment plan and the way the French doctors treated fever patients.

What words would you use to explain how Matilda felt on the morning of October 23?

Matilda's entire world changed in the few months between the beginning and end of this book. Recall the words you used to depict her at the beginning of the story. How would you describe her now?

2. Conclude your work on the biography and add it to the portfolio.

When the Land Belonged to God by Charles Marion Russell

LESSON 61

1. Read pages 327-329 and 345-349 of *George Washington's World*. Discussion and narration prompts:

Maria Jay exemplifies how life changed for many young women in the new republic. Describe this change.

The peaceful transfer of power from one elected president to his elected successor is a hallmark of American democracy. Why do you think this is so important? Why did people cry when Washington left his office willingly to John Adams?

2. George Washington died at the end of 1799, just before the dawn of a new century that would see the nation he helped found grow in amazing ways and face its greatest crisis. John Adams, the second president, served the country in that role for one term. The reasons he lost the election for a second term center around the XYZ Affair and the passage of the Alien and Sedition Acts. Learn more by watching "John Adams Presidency: The XYZ Affair, Alien and Sedition Acts | History with Ms. H" on the History with Ms. H YouTube channel.

3. Thomas Jefferson, following the debacle of the XYZ Affair and ensuing legislation, defeated John Adams and took office in 1801. Introduce *Abraham Lincoln's World* and look over pages 1-3. Read pages ix-x and 11-14.

4. Using the map on page 85 as a guide, shade in the area represented by the Louisiana Purchase on your map of North America.

LESSON 62

1. We will now study Lewis and Clark and their historic expedition by reading *Of Courage Undaunted, Across the Continent with Lewis & Clark* by James Daugherty. This book captures the expedition's energy, spirit, and courage and is based on Lewis and Clark's journals. This makes it an essential work of historical record. It also means that it is limited in its perspective and conveys attitudes towards the Native Americans that are harsh and sometimes shocking. We included this book for several reasons. At this point in the study, you have read books written from the Native perspective and have worked to understand the complexities of colonial and Native relationships. *Of Courage Undaunted* provides a window into how most Americans viewed the Indigenous peoples of America for most of our country's history. This gives you an opportunity to read critically and to be on the lookout for demeaning and dehumanizing language. We will also see how perspectives and narratives shift over time. The authentic courage and curiosity of the Corps of Discovery will be seen alongside their feelings of superiority and cultural blindness. As you read this book, consider whose viewpoints are missing. What would the various tribe members have thought of this group of strange men making their way through their lands? How might Sacajawea have felt? What do Lewis and Clark's words about the Natives reveal about their own characters? How did the author use language to dehumanize the Native tribes to justify American claims to these lands? Developing the ability to ask and answer these questions is a crucial part of becoming a historian! It is also essential to cultivating the ability to see the Imago Dei in all people and recognize that we are all children of God.

Parental Warning: This book contains repeated use of the word squaw. It is historically accurate as Lewis and Clark used it in their journals, and it was not considered denigrating in the early 19th century. Today many Native Americans find it deeply offensive. To better understand how "squaw" has evolved from a descriptive word to become an insult, read the following article: https://indiancountrytoday.com/archive/the-word-squaw-offensive-or-not. The article's content is not intended for children, but it is helpful in discussing the use of this word as you engage in this portion of the study. Another useful article traces the history of this word in English use: http://www.lewis-clark.org/article/336

Lesson continued on next page.

LESSON 62 continued

2. Read Part 1, pages 1-31 of *Of Courage Undaunted*. Discussion and narration prompts:

Thomas Jefferson's recommendation of Meriwether Lewis (page 7) outlines the young man's skills and character qualities. Which attributes stand out to you?

Page 13 contains a description of the author's perspective on what makes an American man. Do you think this is accurate for men in 1803? What about today?

Page 18 refers to "Indian-infested wilderness," and page 25 asks the question, "What did all the vast wilderness between contain? No one knew." How does this sort of language and assertion dehumanize the people who had been living in the "vast wilderness" for hundreds of years? What does this tell you about how Americans viewed the Native populations? As you read through this, notice the adjectives used to describe the Indigenous peoples. Are they generally positive or negative?

3. Begin a new section in the portfolio titled "The Lewis and Clark Expedition."

4. The following website provides information on the Native tribes and nations that the Corps of Discovery encountered along their journey. Refer to it throughout this section to learn more about these civilizations: www.lewis-clark.org/channel/59

LESSON 63

1. Read Part II, pages 32-61 in *Of Courage Undaunted*. Discussion and narration prompts:

Pretend you've joined the Corps of Discovery. Describe the feelings you would be experiencing as you set out on this expedition to a place you knew nothing about, for an undetermined period of time, with people you did not know, and with the genuine possibility of experiencing enemy attacks, sickness, accidents, or even death. What makes you jump at this opportunity? What makes you want to turn back? Record your thoughts in the portfolio.

Captain Lewis described President Jefferson as "the Great White Father" when he met with the Otoe tribe. What did this reveal about the Americans' thoughts about the Natives? Did they view the Otoe as an equal sovereign nation, able to provide for its own governance? Did Lewis attempt to understand the reasons behind the conflict between the Otoes and the Mahas?

The Corps managed to avoid coming into conflict with the Sioux, and the author states, "This took a more difficult kind of courage than actual fighting." (See page 50.) What do you think the author meant by this? Describe another situation where this would be true.

2. Scalping has long been described as something Native tribes did to white settlers, but the history of scalping is much broader and stretches back to ancient Greece. Dutch settlers of New Amsterdam (now New York) were paid bounties for Native scalps. Scalping practices varied by region and culture in North America. If desired, research the history of scalping and record your findings in the notebook.

3. Mark the following landmarks on the map of North America and start tracing the Corps of Discovery's path across the continent. Also, mark the Native nations' territories. The map on pages 164-165 in *Of Courage Undaunted* will be helpful, as will the map to the **right.**

St. Louis, Missouri	Missouri River	St. Charles, Missouri
Platte River	Otoe Territory	Missouri Territory
Omaha Territory	Pawnee Territory	Sioux Territory
Arikara Territory	Mandan Territory	Minatree Territory

William Clark

Meriwether Lewis

LEWIS AND CLARK
EXPEDITION
1804-1806

Lewis and Clark Reach Shoshone Camp Led by Sacajawea by Charles Marion Russell

LESSON 64

1. Read Part III, pages 62-98 in *Of Courage Undaunted*. Narration and discussion prompts:

Narrate Captain Lewis's 31st birthday journal entry (page 96). What did this tell us about the inner life of Meriwether? Did you find any aspect of it surprising? Why or why not?

Describe the reunion of Sacajawea and her brother. How did this event give Lewis a fuller picture of Sacajawea's humanity?

2. Continue charting the Corps of Discovery's progress on the map of North America. Mark their portage around the Great Missouri Falls to White Bear Islands. The following website has a helpful map:
    https://visitgreatfallsmontana.org/trip-ideas/lewis-and-clark-heritage-trail/

Mark the following:

Fort Mandan	Maria's River	Missouri Falls
White Bear Islands	Continental Divide	Yellowstone River
Shoshone Territory	Crow Territory	Blackfeet Territory

3. The Corps of Discovery was responsible for documenting dozens of plants and animals. Visit the following site to see some of these and sketches from Lewis and Clark's journals.
    https://lewisandclarkjournals.unl.edu/images/plants_animals

4. Read more about the Continental Divide here: www.lewis-clark.org/article/1779

LESSON 65

1. Read Part IV, pages 99-123 in *Of Courage Undaunted*. **Note:** Lewis and Clark use European names to refer to the tribes in this section. Discussion and narration prompts:

At the beginning of this book, you imagined what it felt like to be a member of the Corps of Discovery on the day of departure. Now, describe what that brave soul would have felt when he first saw the Pacific Ocean.

When researching these people groups and marking their territories, the following information will be helpful:
    Flathead = Salish and Kootenai
    Chopunnish/Nez Perce or Pierced Noses = Nimiipuu or Ni-mee-poo
    Snake = Northern Paiute, Bannock, and Shoshone

2. Continue charting the Corps of Discovery's progress on the map of North America. Mark the following:

Bitterroot Mountains	Snake (Kooskooskee) River	Rocky Mountains
Fort Rock	Mount Hood	Columbia River
Fort Clatsop	Pacific Ocean	Nimiipuu Territory
Chinook Territory	Salish and Kootenai Territory	

3. Throughout North America, Native populations created vast trade networks, and the expedition members were beneficiaries of the knowledge that passed along these pathways. One small detail from Sergeant John Ordway's journal hints at the complexity of these networks. It offers cultural insights into the value systems of both the Nez Perce and the American cultures. Read more here:
    www.lewis-clark.org/article/3410

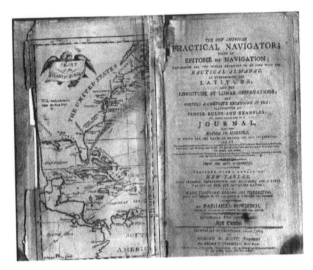

1. Frontispiece of 1802 first edition of Nathaniel Bowditch's *American Practical Navigator*.
2. *Nathaniel Bowditch* by Charles Osgood, 1835 3. *USS Constitution vs Guerriere* by Michel Felice Corne

LESSON 66

1. Read Part V, pages 124-166 in *Of Courage Undaunted*.

Daugherty's tribute to Sacajawea on page 154 captures her quiet strength and dignity. What would you add to his description?

2. Chart the Corps of Discovery's return journey on the map of North America. Use the map on page 85 as a guide.

3. Conclude your study of the Corps of Discovery by writing a press release announcing the explorers' return. Describe the journey, their interactions with the nations they encountered and how Sacajawea aided them, the natural wonders they documented, and any other aspect of the expedition that sparked your interest. Add your press release to the portfolio.

4. PBS has produced a two-part documentary on the Lewis and Clark expedition. You may access it at the following link or check your library for DVDs:
　　www.pbs.org/video/lewis-clark-lewis-and-clark-journey-corps-discovery/

LESSON 67

1. While the Corps was extending the boundaries of the frontier, the young nation was growing and facing challenges at home and abroad. Read pages 15-18 and 22-31 of *Abraham Lincoln's World*. Discussion and narration prompts:

President Madison said the following about the conflict between the pro-war and anti-war factions: "In both parties, I find worthy and intelligent men with honest hearts, enlightened minds and bitter prejudices." Discuss Madison's ability to give both sides respect. He, in the words of Shannon McMahon, "Listened to learn, not to debate." What current political issue comes to mind in which you can describe both sides like Madison? Where might you try to listen to learn?

Tecumseh and the Prophet waged a valiant resistance against the onslaught of American settlers. Compare and contrast Tecumseh and the Prophet's vision with that of the Peacemaker and Hiawatha. What strategies did they employ in their fight for survival that were similar but worked themselves out differently?

2. At this time in history, a young man in Massachusetts had already faced disappointment and tragedy in his life. He would go on to revolutionize navigation science despite never graduating from school. Introduce *Carry On, Mr. Bowditch* by Jean Lee Latham. Read Chapters 1-4. This book tells the story of Bowditch's remarkable life and re-creates what life was like for many people in New England in the early 19th century.

3. Familiarity with the parts of a ship will be helpful for your reading in *Carry On, Mr. Bowditch*. Use the following website for reference: https://classicsailor.com/2019/11/the-fully-rigged-ship/

LESSON 68

1. Read Chapters 5-10 of *Carry On, Mr. Bowditch*. Discussion and narration prompts:

Describe the circumstances that led to Nat's indenture.

What challenges did Nat have to overcome in his young life?

2. The sailing industry formed the backbone for shipping, whaling, trade, and national security in the 19th century. Learn more about the multifaceted marine industry:
　　https://americanhistory.si.edu/onthewater/exhibition/2_3.html

3. Read pages 32-39 of *Abraham Lincoln's World*.

LESSON 69

1. Read Chapters 11-15 of *Carry On, Mr. Bowditch*. Discussion and narration prompts:

> The Essex Almanac stated the following regarding freedom of the press:
> "The Press is dangerous in a despotic government, but in a free country it is very useful, so long as it is free; for it is very important that people should be told everything that concerns them. If we argue against any branch of liberty, just because sometimes people abuse that liberty, then we argue against liberty itself. In a free country, the press must be free."

> Discuss this idea, both historically and now. Do you think freedom of the press includes the right to print or spread lies? Why or why not? And what is the effect this has on liberty?

> Why was Nat so passionate about the accuracy of navigation tables? How had his family's losses shaped this desire for better information?

2. To learn more about Nathaniel Bowditch and his contributions to science and navigation, the following site offers a collection of articles featuring the great American:
> https://nshof.org/inductees/bowditch-nathaniel/

> If you would like to map Bowditch's voyages, check out:
> www.learn4yourlife.com/carry-on-mr-bowditch-maps.html

LESSON 70

1. Read Chapters 16-20 of *Carry On, Mr. Bowditch*.

2. Read pages 47-48 and 55-59 of *Abraham Lincoln's World* to learn more about the War of 1812. "The War of 1812 - Crash Course U.S. History #11" on the CrashCourse YouTube channel provides a snarky summary of the events leading up to this war and its effects that is helpful. Write an overview of the War of 1812 and add it to your portfolio.

3. One of the most enduring tales of the War of 1812 is the burning of Washington, D.C. Read more here:
> www.mountvernon.org/george-washington/artwork/dolley-madison-comes-to-the-rescue/

LESSON 71

1. Finish reading *Carry On, Mr. Bowditch*. Discussion and narration prompts:

> Narrate Nat's discussion with Dr. Holyoke on his experiences with people resisting the smallpox vaccination and sailors rebuffing Bowditch's methods as "book sailing."

> Describe Dr. Bowditch's contribution to the art of navigation.

2. Read pages 65-82 of *Abraham Lincoln's World*.

3. Following the Revolutionary War, new states rapidly joined the original 13 colonies. On your map of North America, add the outlines of the following states, along with the date of their admission to the union:

Vermont: March 4, 1791
Kentucky: June 1, 1792
Tennessee: June 1, 1796
Ohio: March 1, 1803
Louisiana: April 30, 1812
Indiana: December 11, 1816

Mississippi: December 10, 1817
Illinois: December 3, 1818
Alabama: December 14, 1819
Maine: March 15, 1820
Missouri: August 10, 1821

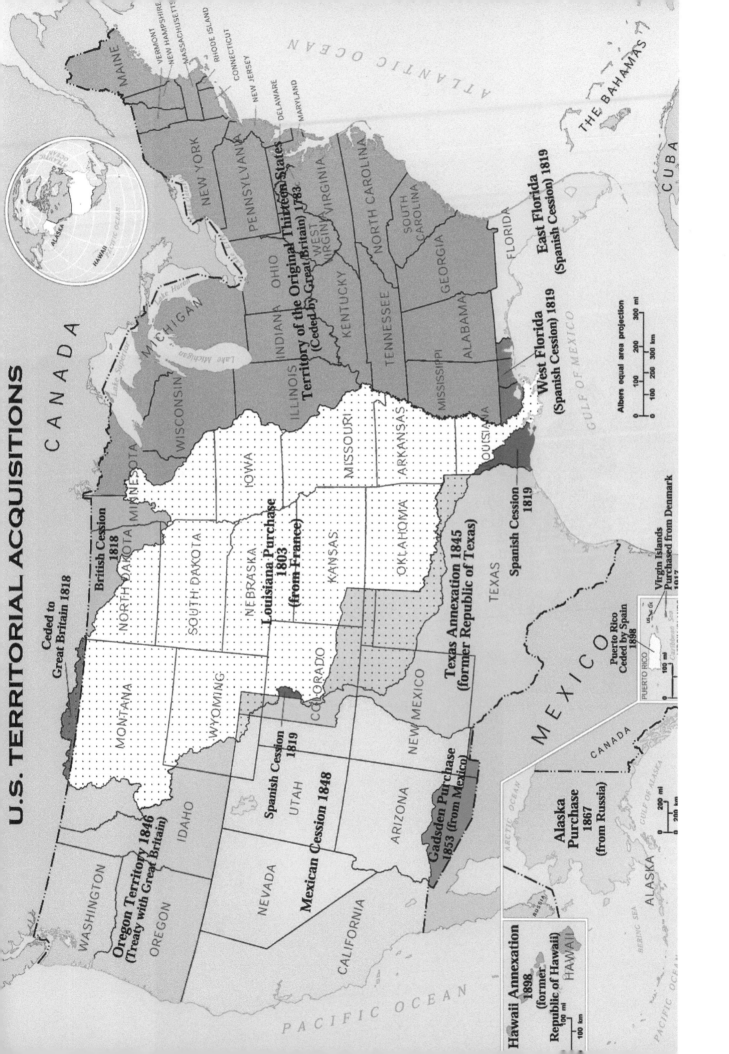

U.S. TERRITORIAL ACQUISITIONS

Tuko-See-Mathla
Seminole chief, c. 1843

Se-loc-ta
Muscogee Creek leader, c. 1838

Sequoyah
Creator of Cherokee syllabary, c. 1830

LESSON 72

1. Read pages 83-102 of *Abraham Lincoln's World*. This section will introduce some history of Mexico that will be important for understanding the United States' historical relationship with our southern neighbor. Discussion and research prompts:

Discuss Andrew Jackson's invasion of the Spanish territory of Florida.

Describe why Chief Justice John Marshall's decision in *Gibbons v. Ogden* was so important. Learn more here: www.quimbee.com/cases/gibbons-v-ogden

What was the Monroe Doctrine? More details here: www.c-span.org/classroom/document/?7151

The Industrial Revolution changed everything about manufacturing, and it also significantly impacted family life. As Sara Hale observed, the family unit was increasingly split. In agricultural cultures, families operated together, men and women laboring together in the fields. As more and more men began working in industry and cities drew people away from family farms, the home increasingly became the domain of women. Discuss how Sara Hale helped shape this new role for women.

2. Using the map on page 91, mark the acquisition of Florida in 1819 on the map of North America.

3. Learn more about the Florida Seminoles, Black Seminoles, and Florida's remarkable history at the following links:

https://fortmose.org/about-fort-mose/
www.thoughtco.com/black-seminoles-4154463
www.semtribe.com/stof/history/timeline

LESSON 73

1. Read pages 115-116, 123-128, and 137-142 of *Abraham Lincoln's World*. Discussion prompts:

Discuss the passionate support and defense of Andrew Jackson as president. Are there any politicians today or in recent memory who evoke similar responses? How are these 21st-century figures similar to or different from the 19th-century president?

Discuss states' historical and recent tendency to threaten "leaving the country" when their interests are not recognized on the federal level. Do states have the "right" to leave the union? Research this and record your findings in the portfolio.

2. Andrew Jackson oversaw several "Indian removals," the most notorious being the Trail of Tears, which occurred in 1838-1839 and he signed into law before he left office. To learn more about the background of the Trail of Tears, watch "Trail of Tears National Historic Trail" on the NationalTrailsNPS YouTube channel.

3. Introduce *Mary and the Trail of Tears: A Cherokee Removal Survival Story*. Read Chapters 1-3. Narration and discussion prompts:

Discuss how Congress's acceptance of the illegal Cherokee Treaty that the Supreme Court had struck down was a violation of the separation of powers.

Margaret stated on page 20, "Words can destroy nations. But they can build nations too." Discuss how this happens, both in the creation and destruction of nations. Can you think of any current examples of this?

LESSON 74

1. Read Chapters 4-6 of *Mary and the Trail of Tears*.

2. Create a new section in the portfolio titled "The Trail of Tears."

3. Mark New Echota (near present-day Calhoun, Georgia) on the map of North America. Learn more about the former capital of the Cherokee Nation here: www.allthingscherokee.com/new-echota/

4. Sequoyah's creation of the Cherokee syllabary was a remarkable achievement. Learn more here: www.pbslearningmedia.org/resource/midlit11.soc.ush.cheralph/the-cherokee-alphabet/

LESSON 75

1. Finish reading *Mary and the Trail of Tears*. Discussion and narration prompts:

> Mary and her family experienced heartbreaking loss when forced from their home and put into the prison camp. The hardship continued for months as they waited and then walked nearly 1000 miles to a strange new place they were expected to make their home. Based on your reading, what do you think motivated them to keep going? How did they maintain their courage despite continued cruelty and adversity?

> Which moments brought momentary relief from the continuous onslaught of suffering?

2. Using the map on page 107 of *Mary and the Trail of Tears*, mark the routes of the Trail of Tears on the map of North America, along with the names of the forts, cities, and rivers on the paths.

3. The Cherokee Nation, despite all the obstacles it faced, established itself anew in Oklahoma. Learn more about how the Cherokee preserve their traditions and pass on this knowledge to future generations by watching "Diligwa, A Living Cherokee History" on the OsiyoTV YouTube channel.

LESSON 76

1. Read pages 143-145, 158-167 of *Abraham Lincoln's World*. Narration and discussion prompts:

> Why do you think the United States was unwilling to follow the example of Great Britain in finding a way to end slavery without a civil war?

2. The practice of slavery increasingly divided the nation. The tide of public sentiment regarding the institution was shifting. Abolitionists like Frederick Douglass were key figures behind this change. We will now read the story of one of the great American abolitionists. Introduce *Sojourner Truth, Ain't I a Woman?* Read the Introduction and Chapters 1-3. **Parental Warning:** This book contains primary source quotations that include racial epitaphs and depictions of brutality.

> Belle's enslaver, Colonel Hardenbergh, only spoke Dutch to his slaves. Discuss how this was one more way he controlled the people he enslaved.

> Baumfree and Mau Mau bore an unimaginable burden as enslaved people. Baumfree had had two previous wives sold away from him. Mau Mau and Baumfree together had 10 children, all of whom were sold as young boys and girls. They were cruelly treated at the end of their long faithful service to the Hardenbergh family, left to freeze and starve. Discuss why you think the Hardenberghs were able to justify this cruelty. Discuss how enslavers had the power to destroy enslaved families.

> Belle's parents could not pass on anything material to their children, but Mau Mau passed on her faith to her daughter. Discuss how Belle's faith strengthened her during unimaginably difficult circumstances.

3. Create a new section of the portfolio titled "Slavery and the Abolitionist Movement."

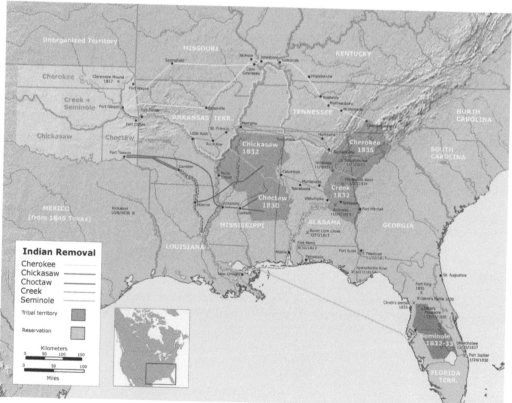

1. *Trail of Tears* mural by Elizabeth Jane, 1938
2. Trail of Tears routes

LESSON 77

1. Read Chapters 4-5 of *Sojourner Truth, Ain't I a Woman?* Discussion and narration prompts:

Narrate the story of the reunion between Belle and her siblings. What discovery came out of that meeting?

One of the injustices of slavery was the ignorance it perpetrated upon the enslaved. How do you think a lack of education, training in critical reasoning, and illiteracy influenced Belle's susceptibility to con artists? Why do you think Benjamin and Ann Folgers decided that Belle would be their scapegoat for the failure of The Kingdom instead of the actual charlatans who had deceived everyone?

Discuss Belle's statement: "The rich rob the poor and the poor rob one another." Why do you think she had this perspective?

What do you think of the names Belle chose for herself?

2. Learn more about the Underground Railroad, its mythology, and how the narrative of enslaved people heading north is incomplete by watching "The Underground Railroad: Crash Course Black American History #15" on the CrashCourse YouTube channel. Discussion prompt:

Dr. Clint Smith challenges us to "sit in the discomfort" of our nation's relationship with slavery. What do you think he means by this? Consider this in light of Winston Churchill's warning, "Those that fail to learn from history are doomed to repeat it." How can minimizing the dark parts of the past lead to their repetition?

3. Explore the remarkable and heroic life of William Still here:
   http://stillfamily.library.temple.edu/exhibits/show/william-still

LESSON 78

1. Read Chapters 6-8 of *Sojourner Truth, Ain't I a Woman?* Narration and discussion prompts:

The African Methodist Episcopal Church hymn on page 79 explores the power of renaming. Given the history of enslaved people bearing their master's names, discuss the spiritual impact they would have felt when singing this hymn. Discuss how former slaves may have understood Revelation 2:17 and Isaiah 56:5 uniquely.

Discuss how the motto of William Lloyd Garrison's newspaper, *The Liberator*, ("No union with slaveholders") foreshadowed the coming rift in the nation.

Discuss how Sojourner rebuffed all attempts to dehumanize and degrade her and her work. How did she use the truth to expose lies?

2. The Dred Scott decision had far-reaching consequences in U.S. history. Learn more by watching "The Dred Scott Decision: Crash Course Black American History #16" on the CrashCourse YouTube channel.

Key Abolitionists

Harriet Beecher Stowe

Harriet Tubman

Sojourner Truth

William Lloyd Garrison

Frederick Douglass

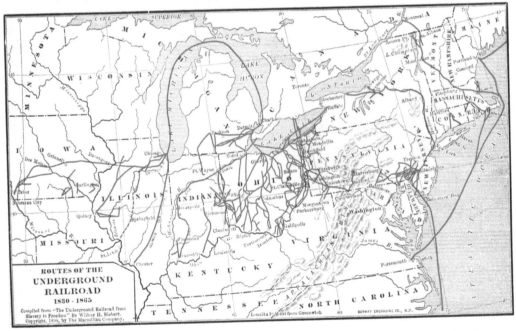

1. *A Ride for Liberty - The Fugitive Slaves* by Eastman Johnson 2. Routes of the Underground Railroad

LESSON 79

1. Finish reading *Sojourner Truth, Ain't I a Woman?*

2. Sojourner Truth's itinerant preaching and abolitionist activity helped shift public opinion on slavery. It is difficult to overstate the importance of her influence. Imagine hosting a dinner party with Sojourner Truth and several of her friends (see pages 165-178 of *Sojourner Truth, Ain't I a Woman?* for inspiration). Write out a description of the party and menu, and create a dialogue. Record in the portfolio.

3. Watch "*Uncle Tom's Cabin* - influence of the Fugitive Slave Act," "*Uncle Tom's Cabin* - plot and analysis," and "*Uncle Tom's Cabin* - reception and significance" on khanacademy.org to learn more about *Uncle Tom's Cabin*, how the Great Awakening influenced it, and how it changed the nation.

LESSON 80

1. Read pages 168-174, 179, and 191-195 of *Abraham Lincoln's World*.

2. Using the map on page 91, shade in the area represented by the Texas Annexation of 1845 and the Oregon Territory of 1846 on the map of North America.

3. Learn more about the Mexican-American War by watching "The Mexican-American War | AP US History | Khan Academy" on the Khan Academy YouTube channel.

4. New states entering the union were a key point of contention for the United States as they grappled with slavery. On the map of North America, add the outlines of the following states, along with the date of their admission to the union:

Arkansas: June 15, 1836
Michigan: January 26, 1837
Florida: March 3, 1845
Texas: December 29, 1845
Iowa: December 28, 1846
Wisconsin: May 29, 1848

California: September 9, 1850
Minnesota: May 11, 1858
Oregon: February 14, 1859
Kansas: January 29, 1861
West Virginia: June 20, 1863
Nevada: October 31, 1864

LESSON 81

1. Read pages 198-215 of *Abraham Lincoln's World*.

2. Begin working on your concluding report. Choose one figure from our study that you believe embodies all the best qualities of what it means to be an American. Begin researching this person and gathering evidence to support your choice.

LESSON 82

1. Read pages 223-225, 242-251, 274-283, and 290-296 of *Abraham Lincoln's World*. This is where our study concludes. Feel free to continue reading *Abraham Lincoln's World* to familiarize yourself with the Civil War. Check out our *Modern American and World History: A Literature Approach for Intermediate Grades* or our *Modern U.S. and World History: A Literature Approach for High School* teachers guides, which cover the Civil War in depth and continue through the early 21st century.

2. Conclude research for your essay and write a persuasive position paper explaining why you chose the person you did to represent the ideals of the United States. Present your report to your family or class and add it to your portfolio.

IN CONCLUSION

"If you would understand anything, observe its beginning and its development."

ARISTOTLE

*T*his journey through the early vast history of our nation, stretching back to Native nations and continuing up to the cusp of the Civil War, is valuable in helping us understand what it means to be an American.

The great men and women in our nation's history were those who held up a mirror to our national conscience to show us where we could do better. They were the people who fought injustice, who used their giftings to save lives, and who shared their stories to change history. The Iroquois who sought a way of peace, the Pilgrims who uprooted their lives to worship freely, the founding fathers who refused to set up another monarchy while setting down words that would serve to continually draw out our better angels, the abolitionists who recognized that the liberty of an entire people group was more important than states' rights, and so many other brave souls reveal the best of our nation. In every era throughout history, injustice and violence rear their ugly heads. Still, our task is not to grow weary but to draw on the examples of Hiawatha, William Bradford, Pocahontas, Sojourner Truth, Nathaniel Bowditch, the Black soldiers who fought for the independence of our nation only to be denied their freedom, and many, many other brave souls who took our nation's founding principles seriously and devoted their lives to ensuring that all people are guaranteed the rights to "life, liberty, and the pursuit of happiness."

Theirs was not a momentary work but the labor of decades, sometimes a lifetime. They were united in their shared call to make our nation better for all who lived here. They devoted themselves to serving others, to causes greater than themselves. Each of these figures walked in humility and pursued justice, and we all benefit from their sacrifice and devotion. Let us follow in their footsteps as we take part in the ongoing task of shaping our "more perfect union."

Additional Resources

For those of you who would like to add a world history component to your early American history study, these charts are provided for Genevieve Foster's "World" books. On the following charts, you will see the pages that are not assigned to be read in the lessons. If you would like to add European history, assign the pages referring to Europe. If you would like to include a basic world history overview, assign all pages in the following charts.

The World of Capt. John Smith

	Europe	Asia	S. America	Africa
PART I: 1580-1598				
1-3 *Overview: People & Events*				
12-20	✔			
23-31	✔			
41-51	✔			
55-64	✔			
69-84	✔			
PART II: 1600-1607				
91-93 *Overview: People & Events*				
94-115		✔		
116-123	✔			
126-135	✔			
143	✔			
144-149		✔		
154-165	✔			
170-172	✔			
PART III: 1607-1620				
199-201 *Overview: People & Events*				
242	✔			
243-253	✔			
260-268	✔	✔		
274-277	✔			
PART IV: 1620-1631				
299-301 *Overview: People & Events*				
316-320	✔	✔		
325-342	✔			
347-362	✔	✔		
372-383	✔			

George Washington's World

	Europe	Asia	S. America	Africa
PART I: 1740-1755				
1-3 *Overview: People & Events*				
28-29				✔
30-38	✔			
39-41		✔		
42-56	✔			
PART II: 1756-1763				
63-65 *Overview: People & Events*				
66-72		✔		
101-103	✔			
104-107		✔		
108-110	✔			
PART III: 1763-1776				
111-113 *Overview: People & Events*				
119-121	✔			
130-135	✔			
139-153	✔	✔		
158-160				✔
PART IV: 1776-1783				
181-183 *Overview: People & Events*				
195-197	✔			
225-227	✔			

	Europe	Asia	S. America	Africa

PART V: 1783 - 1789

PART VI: 1789-1799

Abraham Lincoln's World

	Europe	Asia	S. America	Africa
PART I: 1800-1815				
1-3 Overview: People & Events				
4-10	✔			
19-21	✔		✔	
40-43			✔	
44-46	✔	✔		
49-54	✔			
60-64	✔			
PART II: 1815-1830				
66-67 Overview: People & Events				
103-104				✔
105-114	✔			
117-122	✔	✔		
129-136	✔			
PART III: 1830-1848				
144-145 Overview: People & Events				
146-157	✔	✔		✔
175-190	✔	✔		
196-197	✔			✔
216-222	✔			

	Europe	Asia	S. America	Africa

3 Branches of Government

The Constitution of the United States provides a separation of powers among the three branches of government: Legislative, Executive, and Judicial

Legislative
Makes the Law

Congress

Senate
100 elected senators total; two senators per state

House of Representatives
435 elected representatives total; representation based on each state's population

Executive
Carries out the Law

President

Vice President

Cabinet
Nominated by the President and must be approved by the Senate (with at least 51 votes)

Judicial
Evaluates the Law

Supreme Court
Nine justices nominated by the President and must be approved by the Senate (with at least 51 votes)

Other Federal Courts

Checks and Balances

Executive

Legislative

Judicial

> Can impeach & remove the President from office
> Can override presidential veto
> Declare war, ratify treaties, control appropriations

Veto bills
Recommend legislation
Call special session of Congress

Declare presidential acts unconstitutional
Judges appointed by the President serve for life

> Nominates judges to fill vacancies
> Grants reprieves and pardons

Interprets law and may declare laws unconstitutional <

> Can impeach Judges
> Can refuse judicial appointments
> Can propose constitutional amendments to overrule Supreme Court decisions

US Legislative Process

Every bill starts as an idea that must be approved by both chambers of Congress and signed by the President before it becomes a law.

House of Representatives

A bill is introduced by a member of the House and assigned to a committee for review.

The committee meets to discuss, amend, and vote on the bill.

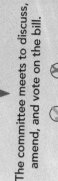

If approved, bill proceeds to the full House for further discussion, amendments, and voting.

Bill must pass through both chambers before being sent to the President.

A conference committee, made of members of both chambers, meets to resolve any differences between the House and Senate versions of the bill.

Both chambers vote on final bill

Senate

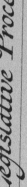

A bill is introduced by a member of the Senate and assigned to a committee for review.

The committee meets to discuss, amend, and vote on the bill.

If approved, bill proceeds to the full Senate for further discussion, amendments, and voting.

President

The President vetoes the bill and sends it back to congress.

The veto can be overridden by Congress with a 2/3 vote.

The President signs the bill and it becomes a law.

Image Credits

Pages 6-7
Sinagua dwelling at Montezuma Castle National Monument, Camp Verde, Arizona © Fotoluminate LLC/ Adobe Stock

Page 10: Indian Basket © James Phelps JR/ Adobe Stock

Page 12
1. Iroquois Five Nations, R. A. Nonenmacher, Public domain, via Wikimedia Commons
2. Iroquois Leaders, 1570, Public domain, via Wikimedia Commons.

Page 15
Native cultures map, https://lochgarry.wordpress.com/2011/11/27/ancient-winds-and-memories-of-a-time-long-ago/
Accessed 10/13/2021

Page 16
1. Battle between Iroquois and Algonquin tribes near Lake Champlain
as drawn by Samuel de Champlain, Public domain, via Wikimedia Commons
2. Iroquois with western goods pictured in *Histoire de l'Amérique septentrionale: divisée en quatre tomes* by Bacqueville de la Potherie, Public domain, via Wikimedia Commons

Page 18
1. Traditional Native American Food © quadxeon / Adobe Stock
2. The Three Sisters © Rea Berg, 2020

Pages 20-21: Fortifications at Jamestown © Zack Frank / Adobe Stock

Pages 24: *Incolarum Virginiae piscandi ratio* Theodor de Bry after John White, ca. 1590, Public domain.

Page 27
1. Powhatan statue in bronze © spiritofamerica / Adobe Stock
2. Capt. John Smith, engraver uncertain - Houghton Library, Public domain, via Wikimedia Commons.
3. Artist conception of aerial view of Jamestown, Virginia 1614 by Sidney King - https://casc.usgs.gov/content/safeguarding-our-cultural-past-future-climate-change-scientists-work-protect-cultural, Public domain, via Wikimedia Commons.

Page 30: *The Mayflower*, artist unknown © mheston / Adobe Stock

Page 33
1. *Pilgrims Going to Church* by George Henry Boughton - https://www.nyhistory.org/exhibit/pilgrims-going-church-0, Public Domain, via Wikimedia Commons.
2. © Archivist / Adobe Stock

Page 34: John Smith's map of New England, from *A Description of New England*, 1616. Penobscot Marine Museum, Public domain, via Wikimedia Commons

Page 36-37: *Penn's Treaty with the Indians* by Edward Hicks, Public domain, via Wikimedia Commons

Page 40: Plan of slave ship: By Jbolden030170 - Own work,
CC BY-SA 3.0, https://commons.wikimedia.org/w/index.php?curid=22210919

Page 42
1. Daniel Orme, after W. Denton, Public domain, via Wikimedia Commons
2. *The Life and Adventures of Olaudah Equiano, or, Gustavus Vassa, the African: from an Account Written by Himself to which are Added Some Remarks on the Slave Trade, etc. abridged* by A. Mott (New York: Samuel Wood & Sons, 1829).
Wood engravings by Alexander Anderson (1775-1870) Graphic Arts Collection (GAX) Hamilton 286.
3. Atlantic Trade Triangle by Ryan Maloney for Beautiful Feet Books. ©2021

Page 44
1. Engraving from Voltaire's *Candide*, Jean-Michel Moreau, Public domain, via Wikimedia Commons
2. *Ten Views in the Island of Antigua* by William Clark, c. 1823. British Library, CC0, via Wikimedia Commons

Page 46
1. *Benjamin Franklin*, artist unknown © Archivist / Adobe Stock
2. Sculpture of Benjamin Franklin in Boston, 1856 © ASP Inc / Adobe Stock

Page 49: Frontispiece from *Poems on Various Subjects, Religious and Moral* by Phillis Wheatley.
Yale Collection of American Literature, Beinecke Rare Book and Manuscript Library, Public domain, via Wikimedia Commons.

Page 50
1. *Common Sense*, originally by Thomas Paine. Public domain, via Wikimedia Commons.
2. *Thomas Paine* by Laurent Dabos, Public domain, via Wikimedia Commons

Pages 52-53: *Passage of the Delaware* by Thomas Sully - [2], Public domain, via Wikimedia Commons.

Page 55: *The American Soldiers* by H. Charles McBarron, Jr., Public domain, via Wikimedia Commons

Page 58
1. *Caesar Tarrant*, artist unknown. Public domain.
2. *James Forten* probably by Robert Douglass Jr., Public Domain, via Wikimedia Commons.
3. *Agrippa Hill* by unknown author - https://www.blackpast.org/african-american-history/agrippa-hull-revolutionary-patriot/, Public domain, via Wikimedia Commons.
4. *Lemuel Haynes* by Daggett, Hinman & Co., sc. - Cooley, Timothy Mather. (1837) Sketches of the Life and Character of the Rev. Lemuel Haynes, A.M. Harper & Brothers (New York, NY). Public domain, via Wikimedia Commons
5. *Peter Salem* by Walter J. Williams, Jr. - Revolutionary War Journal, Public Domain, Wikimedia Commons

Page 61
1. *Baron Steuben Drilling Troops at Valley Forge* by Edwin Austin Abbey (1852-1911), Public domain, via Wikimedia Commons
2. *Bunker Hill* by Howard Pyle, Public domain, via Wikimedia Commons

Page 62
1. *John André* by unknown, picture in the London Tower, Public Domain, via Wikimedia Commons.
2. *Capture of Major John André* by John Paulding, David Williams & Isaac Vanwart. Lithograph by J. Baillie, 1845. Public Domain, via Wikimedia Commons.
3. Cipher letter by Benedict Arnold; Peggy Shippen Arnold - From the digital collections of the New York Public Library. Source: Print Collection portrait file. Public domain, via Wikimedia Commons.
4. *Benedict Arnold* by Thomas Hart, 1776. Public domain, via Wikimedia Commons.

Page 65
1. Major campaigns of the Revolutionary War by the United States Military Academy - West Point, Public domain, via Wikimedia Commons

Pages 66-67
The Rocky Mountains, Lander's Peak by Albert Bierstadt, 1863, public domain via Metropolitan Museum of Art, New York, NY

Page 69
Indians Discovering Lewis and Clark by Charles Marion Russell. Public domain, via Wikimedia Commons

Page 72
1. *Washington as Statesman at the Constitutional Convention* by Junius Brutus Stearns, via Wikimedia Commons
2. Assembly room at Independence Hall, Philadelphia © jiawangkun / Adobe Stock

Page 77
States & Territories of the United States of America, March 4, 1789 - August 7, 1789, via Wikimedia Commons

Page 78
1. Elfreth's Alley, in Old City, Philadelphia, Pennsylvania © jonbilous / Adobe Stock
2. *Bush Hill* by James Peller Malcolm, c. 1792. via Wikimedia Commons

Page 80
1. *Richard Allen* by Daniel A. Payne, Public domain, via Wikimedia Commons
2. *Matthew Clarkson*, artist unknown. Scan by NYPL, Public domain, via Wikimedia Commons
3. *Absalom Jones* by Raphaelle Peale, Public domain, via Wikimedia Commons
4. *Benjamin Rush* by Charles Willson Peale, Public domain, via Wikimedia Commons

Page 82
When the Land Belonged to God by Charles Marion Russell, Public domain, via Wikimedia Commons

Page 85
1. *William Clark* by Charles Willson Peale, Public domain, via Wikimedia Commons
2. *Meriwether Lewis* by Charles Willson Peale, Public domain, via Wikimedia Commons
3. Lewis and Clark Expedition map, Victor van Werkhooven, Public domain, via Wikimedia Commons

Pages 86
Lewis and Clark Reach Shoshone Camp Led by Sacajawea by Charles Marion Russell, 1918. Public domain, via Wikimedia Commons

Page 88
1. Frontispiece of 1802 first edition of Nathaniel Bowditch's *American Practical Navigator.* By U.S. Government image from: http://www.usno.navy.mil/library/rare/bowditch.jpg Public Domain, via Wikimedia Commons.
2. *Nathaniel Bowditch* by Charles Osgood, 1835. Image © 2006 Peabody Essex Museum/Photograph by Mark Sexton
3. *USS Constitution vs Guerriere* by Michel Felice Corne. Public Domain, via Wikimedia Commons

Page 91
U.S. Territorial Acquisitions Map, United States federal government (en:User:Black and White converted it from JPEG to PNG and retouched it), Public domain, via Wikimedia Commons

Page 92
1. Bowen, John T., Lithographer, Thomas Loraine McKenney, and James Hall. Tuko-See-Mathla, a Seminole chief / drawn, printed & colored at the Lithographic & Print Colouring Establishment, Phila. Phila.: Published by Daniel Rice & James G. Clark. Photograph. Retrieved from the Library of Congress, <www.loc.gov/item/94504628/>.
2. *Se-Loc-Ta* by Charles Bird King - http://www.si.edu/ahhp/cbking/CB%20King%20Exhibit.htm, Public Domain, via Wikimedia Commons
3. *Sequoyah* by Henry Inman, c. 1830. Public domain, via Wikimedia Commons

Page 95
1. *Trail of Tears* mural by Elizabeth Jane, 1938. Oklahoma History Center.
2. *Trail of Tears*, User:Nikater, Public domain, via Wikimedia Commons

Page 97
1. *Harriet Beecher Stowe* by not specified - This media is available in the holdings of the National Archives and Records Administration, cataloged under the National Archives Identifier (NAID) 535784., Public Domain, via Wikimedia Commons.
2. *Harriet Tubman* by Benjamin F. Powelson - Swann Galleries, Public Domain, via Wikimedia Commons
3. *Sojourner Truth*, circa 1864, by Unknown author - This image is available from the United States Library of Congress's Prints and Photographs division under the digital ID cph.3g06166. Public Domain, via Wikimedia Commons
4. *William Lloyd Garrison* by George Kendall Warren, photographer - Digital Collection of NYPL, Public Domain, via Wikimedia Commons
5. *Frederick Douglass* by George Kendall Warren, photographer. This media is available in the holdings of the National Archives and Records Administration, cataloged under the National Archives Identifier (NAID) 558770., Public Domain, via Wikimedia Commons

Page 98
1. *A Ride for Liberty - The Fugitive Slaves* by Eastman Johnson, Public domain, via Wikimedia Commons
2. *Routes of the Underground Railroad* by http://history.sandiego.edu/gen/CWPics/86139.jpg. Compiled from "The Underground Railroad from Slavery to Freedom" by Wilbur H. Siebert, The Macmillan Company, 1898.[1], Public Domain, via Wikimedia Commons

Pages 100-101
Children holding flags © vectorfusionart LLC/ Adobe Stock